" Long recognized as one of the best CEOs of the 20th century, Bill George has quickly become one " of the foremost authorities on leadership—a wise, no-nonsense author with a large, growing following. This latest book is an excellent practical account of why so many corporate leaders failed and yet others turned crisis into opportunity—and how you can apply those lessons to your own leadership.

—David Gergen, Professor, Director of Center for Public Leadership, Harvard Kennedy School

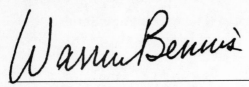

A WARREN BENNIS BOOK

This collection of books is devoted exclusively to new and exemplary contributions to management thought and practice. The books in this series are addressed to thoughtful leaders, executives, and managers of all organizations who are struggling with and committed to responsible change. My hope and goal is to spark new intellectual capital by sharing ideas positioned at an angle to conventional thought—in short, to publish books that disturb the present in the service of a better future.

Books in the Warren Bennis Signature Series

Best-Selling Books by Bill George

Authentic Leadership: Rediscovering the Secrets to Creating Lasting Value

True North: Discover Your Authentic Leadership

Finding Your True North: A Personal Guide

7 LESSONS FOR LEADING IN CRISIS

BILL GEORGE

Author of best-selling *True North*
and *Authentic Leadership*

Foreword by Warren Bennis

JOSSEY-BASS
A Wiley Imprint
www.josseybass.com

Published by Jossey-Bass
A Wiley Imprint
989 Market Street, San Francisco, CA 94103-1741—www.josseybass.com

Jossey-Bass books and products are available through most bookstores. To contact
Jossey-Bass directly call our Customer Care Department within the U.S. at 800-956-7739,
outside the U.S. at 317-572-3986, or fax 317-572-4002.

Jossey-Bass also publishes its books in a variety of electronic formats. Some content that
appears in print may not be available in electronic books.

Library of Congress Cataloging-in-Publication Data
George, Bill (William W.)
  Seven lessons for leading in crisis / by Bill George ; foreword by Warren Bennis.—1st ed.
     p. cm.—(Warren Bennis signature series)
  "A Warren Bennis book"—
  Includes bibliographical references.
  ISBN 978-0-470-53187-7 (cloth)
  1. Crisis management. 2. Leadership. I. Title.
  HD49.G464 2009
  658.4'092—dc22

                                                                    2009021646

Printed in the United States of America
FIRST EDITION
HB Printing   10 9 8 7 6 5 4 3 2 1

*To all the authentic leaders
who are building enduring organizations
that contribute to making this world
a better place to live*

CONTENTS

CONTENTS

ACKNOWLEDGMENTS

This book is the result of encouragement I received from Warren Bennis and Susan Williams of Jossey-Bass to offer a practical guide to leaders about navigating through a crisis. It is based on my personal experiences in the many crises I have witnessed and experienced personally over the years. Warren, Susan, and their colleagues at Jossey-Bass offered a great deal of insight and constructive ideas.

I am also most grateful to the leaders I have known, many of them featured in these pages, who have led their organizations through a wide range of crises that enabled them to emerge stronger as a result. Their willingness to share their insights with me is a great gift to all those emerging leaders who are seeking to use their leadership gifts to make a difference in the world.

During the writing and editing process, I received valuable advice from Nitin Nohria, Penny George, Grace Kahng, Daisy Wademan Dowling, Nick Craig, Tim Dorman, Amy Avergun, Matt Breitfelder, Rye Barcott, Erin White, and

David Gergen. My special appreciation goes to Diane Weinhold, my office manager; Kathy Farren, my assistant at Harvard Business School; and Caitlin Weixel, who helped with the text and the references.

None of this would have been possible without the unwavering support, encouragement, insights, and patience of my wife, Penny, from whom I have learned so much about people and leading them.

THE AUTHOR

Bill George is professor of management practice at Harvard Business School, where he teaches leadership. He was chief executive of Medtronic from 1991 until 2001 and chairman of the board from 1996 to 2002. Under his leadership, Medtronic's market capitalization grew from $1.1 billion to $60 billion, averaging 35 percent a year. He serves on the boards of directors of ExxonMobil and Goldman Sachs and, previously, Novartis and Target Corporation.

He is the author of three best-selling books: *True North: Discover Your Authentic Leadership* (Jossey-Bass, 2007); its companion piece, *Finding Your True North: A Personal Guide* (Jossey-Bass, 2008); and *Authentic Leadership: Rediscovering the Secrets of Creating Lasting Value* (Jossey-Bass, 2003). He has made frequent appearances on television and radio, including the *Charlie Rose Show*, CNBC, the *Today Show*, the *News Hour with Jim Lehrer*, *Bloomberg News*, *Fox Business News*, and national public radio. His articles have appeared in *Fortune Magazine*, the *Wall Street Journal*,

Business Week, Harvard Business Review, and numerous other publications.

He has been named one of Top 25 Business Leaders of the Past 25 Years by PBS; Executive of the Year — 2001 by the Academy of Management; and Director of the Year — 2001–02 by the National Association of Corporate Directors. He is currently a trustee of the Carnegie Endowment for International Peace, World Economic Forum USA, and Tyrone Guthrie Theater. He has been board chair of Allina Health System, Abbott-Northwestern Hospital, United Way of Greater Twin Cities, and Advamed.

Earlier in his career, he was an executive with Honeywell and Litton Industries and served in the U.S. Department of Defense. He has been a professor of leadership at IMD International and executive in residence at the Yale School of Management. He received his B.S. in industrial engineering from Georgia Tech and M.B.A. from Harvard University, where he was a Baker Scholar. He has received honorary doctorates from Georgia Tech and Bryant University.

FOREWORD

"I curse you; may you live in an important age." So went the ancient Chinese imprecation as recounted by Nikos Kazant-zakis in his *Report to Greco*. Could you and I hope to be any more wonderfully cursed than in this turbulent age that we now encounter?

Crisis, says Bill George, is the defining moment for a leader—and in his latest book, he offers a wonderful guide to leadership within such a vexed context. Bill does not offer a blueprint per se. That would not be consistent with who he is. Rather, he helps leaders understand (maybe for the first time) their own inner compasses and to calibrate them to serve as the most reliable instruments for navigating treacherous seas.

He and I are both fond of framing obstacles and grand challenges as "crucible experiences" that are crucial to the refining of leaders who make the greatest impact. I've taken lately to the hopeful notion that our society's emerging adults may even be a "crucible generation," who will be spurred to new heights on account of the failure of their elders. "It is not in the still calm of life or the repose of a pacific station that great characters are formed," Abigail Adams wrote to her son John Quincy in 1780. "The habits of a vigorous mind are formed in contending with difficulty. Great necessities call out great virtues."

Bill indeed views crisis as serendipity—as an inestimable gift that frees leaders to reinvent themselves and their organizations for the long haul. His words carry the special weight of a man who offers an unsurpassed blend of meaningful experience in private industry, government service, and non-profit worlds, along with a rare ability to reflect on his experiences in a manner that can teach others.

Which is why he is a caring and inspirational teacher. He generously calls me in Lesson 2 a mentor to whom he has turned in times of uncertainty. The fact is that I've learned much from Bill over the years. He has helped influence my bottom line on leadership: that it is fundamentally a matter of character. Bill's ability to articulate how leaders can and must discover their sense of True North has been an invaluable contribution to myself and others.

Connecting leadership to character may seem too sentimental a pedagogy in our how-to, technique-obsessed society. In response, I submit the life and lessons of Bill George, which spill forth on the following pages. Bill's integrity and character, forged under pressure, serve as a reality check for all current and aspiring leaders. I would go so far as to argue that strong character is the only means by which a person can even hope to perceive or define reality clearly, rather than through those many illusions and vanities that come undone in moments of stress testing.

Bill not only has his own experiences to offer in this book, but cautionary stories and tales of inspiration from hundreds of organizations and managers he has examined over the years. In moments of trial, some got it right, and many got it wrong, and he captures the upshot in a masterful fashion.

I should offer an important observation about the man who was transformed by identifying and moving toward his personal True North. As detailed in these pages, Bill discerned at a pivotal moment that the direction in which he wanted to move was more important than the hierarchical position he could achieve. He soon moved from being a CEO-in-waiting at a prestigious organization that didn't reflect his passions toward a role at a smaller company that meshed with his deeper sense of purpose.

It's common for most aspiring leaders to be blinded by position, I find, and I marvel at how Bill's life changed once he locked in on his True North. Leadership indeed isn't about position. As the word indicates, it is about moving in a direction, moving meaningfully according to one's compass, with the ability to engage others along the way. Studying the art and adventure of leadership within organizations and societies, in that sense, is quite different from studying raw power or formal institutional authority.

People who are intent on going in a meaningful direction have a chance of finding their way through the fog of crisis and of bringing others alongside them. By contrast, organizations managed by people whose main goal is to preserve their own power or prestige will inevitably founder when crisis beckons. The former type of person will make it through the weather, or will make the weather, if necessary. The latter will blame the fates and other mortals for getting in the way.

In our day, as trillions of dollars of net worth have been turning to ash and as great careers have been imploding and some young careers have been exploding on the launching pad, I think of Marlon Brando's sullen character, Terry Malloy, in *On the Waterfront*. Blaming the collapse of his boxing career on his brother and their unsavory colleagues after he had agreed to a fix a fight, he could only lament: "I coulda been a contender. I coulda been somebody, instead of a bum, which is what I am, let's face it. It was you, Charley." But true leaders accept personal responsibility, do not obsess on past failures, and smell fragrant opportunity in air that is too thin for others.

Bill cites in his concluding chapter a recent book by Jonathan Alter about Franklin D. Roosevelt, America's enduring icon of crisis leadership. It was in fact Alter who offered another remarkable observation about leaders some years earlier. "Anyone can lead where people already want to go," he wrote. "True leaders take them where only their better selves are willing to tread. That's where the leaders' own values come in. They must want to do something with their power, not just be powerful."

Indeed, that's the essence of what Bill teaches us and the essence of what he has lived in this important age that keeps growing confoundingly more important.

June 2009   Warren Bennis
Santa Monica, California

INTRODUCTION: THE ULTIMATE TEST OF LEADERSHIP

There is nothing quite like a crisis to test your leadership. It will make or break you as a leader.

Crises have brought down many leaders and their organizations with them, while other leaders have risen to the challenges to prove their mettle.

What makes leading your organization through difficult situations so hard? Like being in a war, crises test you to your limits because the outcome is rarely predictable. You not only have to use all your wisdom to guide your organization through it, you must dig deep inside yourself to find the courage to keep going forward.

LEADERS DEVELOP THROUGH CRISES

The economic calamity of 2008–2009 was not caused by subprime mortgages, credit default swaps, or even excessive greed. These are only symptoms of the real problem. The root cause of the problem was failed leadership from leaders who didn't follow their True North. In *True North*, I defined True North as the internal compass of your beliefs, values, and principles that guide you through life. Like being in a crucible, a crisis tests whether you will hold fast to your beliefs.

Staying on course is much easier when things are going well. But will you do so under the enormous pressure that comes with a crisis? Can you stay focused on your True North in the face of temptations to bend the rules to get through the crisis? How will you respond when threatened that everything you built for years might be destroyed?

Leaders aligned with their True North are prepared to guide their organizations through severe situations because they know who they are. They have the self-awareness, self-confidence, and resilience to take responsibility for their failings and lead others through the rapidly unfolding—and often unpredictable—sequence of events. They rise to the occasion, find leadership abilities they never knew they had, and come through with shining colors.

An old English proverb says, "A smooth sea never made a skilled mariner." Managing a growing business is a lot easier than leading through difficult times. Growth periods don't test your intestinal fortitude the way a large-scale problem does, nor do they determine whether you will stay on track in the heat of battle. Running a stable business requires discipline and managerial skills, but it doesn't test real leadership capabilities.

Unfortunately, there is no training ground for leading your organization through a crisis short of gaining the experience yourself. M.B.A. programs don't teach you how. Crisis simulation exercises are just that: simulations, not the real thing. Studying cases of leaders in crisis is useful, but you won't know how you will respond until you go through it.

Leaders who never get tested until they reach the top may be unable to cope with the inevitable unforeseen events that come with the job. Some buckle under the pressure. Others become immobilized. Still others make big mistakes but learn from them to become better leaders the next time around.

WHO WILL PASS THE TEST?

Under pressure, some leaders not only pass the test, but their leadership emerges even stronger. That's what happened when Lou Gerstner saved IBM in the mid-1990s and Anne Mulcahy took the helm at Xerox. Inheriting companies facing bankruptcy, they showed great leadership, not just in saving their companies but restoring them to leadership in their respective fields.

To lead their organizations through challenging times as Mulcahy and Gerstner did, leaders have to dig deep inside themselves to gather wisdom and courage. As Jeff Immelt said of the crisis he experienced at GE's plastics business earlier in his career, "Leadership is a long journey into your own soul. At times like these, it's not like anyone can tell you how to do it." Immelt has spoken thoughtfully about the challenges today's CEOs face in trying to address simultaneously the economic crisis, massive technology and globalization changes, short-term financial results, and government intervention.

Sadly, many leaders do not measure up to these challenges. Senior leaders who fail are unlikely to make a comeback. More often than not, they rationalize their failings and blame others while disappearing from genuine leadership responsibilities.

In Chinese, the character for the word *crisis* is made up of two symbols, danger and opportunity. That's exactly what it represents for you as a leader. Although there is always the danger of failing, guiding people through a major problem is your best opportunity to develop your leadership. That's why I recommend that young leaders get down on the playing field early in their careers rather than commenting from the press box.

Young leaders also have the opportunity to learn from their mistakes in order to handle the next crisis by following their True North. David Neeleman got fired at Southwest Airlines but rebounded to create a highly successful airline in JetBlue. Kevin Sharer learned by failing at MCI and became an outstanding CEO at Amgen.

THE GLOBAL ECONOMIC MELTDOWN

There could not be a better testing ground for leaders than the global economic meltdown. On Wall Street, leaders like

J. P. Morgan's Jamie Dimon, Lloyd Blankfein of Goldman Sachs, and John Mack of Morgan Stanley stepped up to the challenge. Chuck Prince of Citigroup, Martin Sullivan of AIG, Lehman's Richard Fuld, and others were unable to cope with the severe pressures.

The origins of the meltdown date back to the 1970s when leading economists like Nobel laureate Milton Friedman advocated that shareholder value should be the primary measure of corporate performance. The instant stock price became the proxy for a corporation's true value. Friedman argued against consideration of the interests of other stakeholders in measuring corporate performance in his landmark 1970 article, labeling those concerned about other stakeholders "pure, unadulterated socialists."

By the mid-1990s Friedman's philosophy had gained widespread popularity. Meeting expectations for quarterly earnings became the primary driver of stock price as corporations were pressured to maximize short-term shareholder value. This pressure caused many managers to sacrifice long-term investments in research and development, customer satisfaction, and market share.

Former General Electric CEO Jack Welch recently offered a contrary point of view. Welch, whose leadership led to an increase of $400 billion in the value of GE stock during his twenty years, argued against focusing on shareholder value. He told the *Financial Times*, "On the face of it, shareholder value is the dumbest idea in the world. Shareholder value is a result, not a strategy. . . . Your main constituencies are your employees, your customers and your products."

FORESHADOWING OF THE CURRENT CRISIS

The failure of hedge fund Long-Term Capital Management (LTCM) in 1998 presaged the global economic meltdown by a decade. Founded in 1994 by investment bankers and Nobel laureates, LTCM used mathematical models to maximize trading gains. In 1998 its high-risk strategies backfired, resulting in $4.5 billion in losses that threatened the fund's collapse. To avoid widespread financial panic, Treasury Secretary Robert Rubin organized fourteen investment banks to create a $3.6 billion bailout of LTCM.

Most Wall Street firms and government officials quickly forgot the lessons of LTCM. The following year Federal Reserve Bank chairman Alan Greenspan and Treasury Secretary Lawrence Summers pushed for the deregulation of financial institutions, including repeal of the 1933 Glass-Steagall Act, which separated commercial banking from investment banking. In the next five years, thousands of unregulated hedge funds were created with no transparency and high-risk strategies eerily similar to those of LTCM.

Collapse of Enron and Arthur Andersen

The collapse of Enron and Arthur Andersen in the fall of 2002, followed by similar problems with WorldCom, Qwest, and Tyco, resulted from high-risk strategies and illegal accounting that triggered passage of the 2003 Sarbanes-Oxley Act. It had the beneficial effect of tightening up corporate accounting and requiring CEOs and board members to attest to the veracity of the numbers. In the following year, over two hundred companies made major accounting restatements.

In *Authentic Leadership*, I wrote that "capitalism became a victim of its own success." I argued, "We need new leadership: authentic leaders, people of the highest integrity, committed to building enduring organizations . . . leaders who have the courage to build their companies to meet the needs of all their stakeholders, and who recognize the importance of their service to society."

Since Enron's fall, a new group of corporate CEOs has emerged who are highly authentic, focused on the long-term health of their companies, and committed to serve the needs of all stakeholders. Many of the leaders profiled in *True North*—Sam Palmisano of IBM, Dan Vasella of Novartis, Andrea Jung of Avon, Indra Nooyi of PepsiCo, and Jeff Immelt of GE, to name just a few—have led their organizations extremely well through the current crisis, although none was immune from the ravages of the stock market decline.

ROOT CAUSE OF GLOBAL ECONOMIC MELTDOWN

With notable exceptions, Wall Street leaders failed to learn from these earlier events. Their high-risk strategies and excessive leverage continued to escalate along with their compensation, reaching a crescendo in 2007. The leaders of failed firms like Bear Stearns, AIG, Lehman Brothers, Countrywide Financial, Fannie Mae, Freddie Mac, Merrill Lynch, Citigroup, Wachovia, and UBS didn't see the crisis coming and were unable to adapt in time to save their firms.

With no restraints from government officials, they kept dancing faster and faster until the music stopped—and the financial collapse followed. According to governance experts Martin Lipton and Jay Lorsch, "Excessive stockholder power is precisely what caused the short-term fixation that led to the current financial crisis. There is a direct causal relationship between the financial meltdown and the short-term focus that drove reckless behavior." This led the Sage of Omaha, Warren Buffett, to observe, "When the tide goes out, you discover who's been swimming naked." Given Buffett's remarkable track record of success, it puzzles me that more investors have not followed his conservative strategies of long-term investments, underlying value analysis, and limited complexity.

Management guru Peter Drucker once said, "Leadership is not rank or privileges, titles or money. Leadership is responsibility." What shocks me is that leaders are not accepting their responsibility for this fiasco, in spite of the trillions of dollars and millions of jobs that have been lost.

Some failed leaders are still in denial, refusing to take responsibility for the missteps that caused their firms to collapse. Former Bear Stearns CEO Alan Schwartz told the *New York Times*, "Looking backwards, if I'd have known exactly the forces that were coming, what actions could we have taken to have avoided this situation? I simply have not been able to come up with anything that would have made a difference." Failed Lehman Brothers CEO Richard Fuld added, "I wake up every single night thinking, what could I have done differently? I made those decisions with the information I had."

Schwartz and Fuld are unwilling to examine honestly their roles in these failures. Which of us who has been responsible for less significant failures couldn't think of many things we would have done differently? In their denial, Schwartz and Fuld are abandoning their responsibilities as leaders.

In his April 2009 address to the Council of Institutional Investors, Goldman Sachs CEO Lloyd Blankfein addressed the broader issues. He acknowledged the financial community's responsibility for the events that precipitated the economic meltdown, noting, "Financial institutions have an obligation to the broader financial system. We depend on a healthy, well functioning system, but we collectively neglected to raise enough questions about whether some of the trends and practices that became commonplace really served the public's long-term interests."

THE 7 LESSONS

What kind of challenges are you facing in your organization? What are the practical ways you can lead your organization through them without being undone? With all the pressures, how do you stay on course of your True North?

This book is aimed at helping leaders at all levels of organizations, from those in the early stages of their careers to recently appointed CEOs. We will examine the issues you are facing in your organization and develop pragmatic approaches that will enable you to answer these questions.

To offer relevant examples, we will examine a wide range of crises that leaders have faced and how they dealt with them. Some of these predicaments were triggered by external events like upheavals in the economy, a run on the company's stock, hostile takeover attempts, and weather and other acts of God. Many more resulted from internal problems, such as product quality and recalls, business ethics and legal issues, earnings shortfalls, accounting scandals, and organizational upheavals.

Most of these examples are drawn from leaders I know personally, as well as my experiences at Medtronic, Honeywell, and Litton Industries and the boards on which I have served: Goldman Sachs, ExxonMobil, Novartis, and Target. I have drawn on these experiences because I have observed these organizations and their leaders firsthand. I also make use of some of the richest cases I have taught at Harvard Business School.

For each example, I offer my firsthand observations about these leaders—what they did right and what they did wrong in handling crises. I hasten to point out that none of them is perfect, and there is no assurance that their future leadership will be as effective as it has been in the past.

From these cases, we will derive the seven lessons that I have gleaned through my years of leading in business, nonprofits, government, and academia. You will be able to apply these lessons immediately in dealing with the predicaments you are facing today and future ones as they arise.

Each of the following seven lessons makes up a chapter of this book. In the Conclusion, I offer my thoughts on your personal leadership and what it takes to follow your True North when you may be facing your defining moment.

Lesson 1: Face reality, starting with yourself. Facing the reality of the crisis is the most important lesson of all. Until you acknowledge that you are facing a serious problem, including your role in creating it, you cannot move forward to solve it.

Lesson 2: Don't be Atlas; get the world off your shoulders. You cannot get through this alone, so don't try to carry the whole world on your shoulders. Reach out to others inside your organization and in your personal life to share the burden and help you come out a winner. This is a great opportunity to strengthen chemistry within your team, because the strongest bonds are built in crisis.

Lesson 3: Dig deep for the root cause. Under the pressures of a crisis, there is temptation to jump to quick-fix solutions that may mask the real problems and leave your organization vulnerable to repeating the crisis. The only way to solve these problems is to understand their root cause and implement permanent solutions.

Lesson 4: Get ready for the long haul. When you are confronting significant problems, your first reaction may be that things can't really be that bad. But in its early stages, you may be looking only at the tip of the iceberg, and things may get a lot worse. In a crisis, cash becomes king. To survive the crisis, you need to prepare for a long struggle to defend against the worst conditions so you will be prepared to pass through the eye of the storm.

Lesson 5: Never waste a good crisis. The challenges you are facing represent your best opportunity to make major changes in your organization because they lessen the resistance that exists in good times. You should move aggressively to take actions necessary to strengthen your organization as you emerge from it.

Lesson 6: You're in the spotlight: Follow True North. In a crisis, everyone watches what you do. Whether you like it or not, you are in the spotlight both inside and outside the company. Will you stay focused on your True North, or will you succumb to the pressure?

Lesson 7: Go on offense; focus on winning now. Coming out of a crisis, the market never looks the same as it did going in. So don't just batten down the hatches and wait for business to come back. This is your opportunity to reshape the market to play to your strengths. While others are licking their wounds, you should focus on winning now.

These seven lessons will be useful immediately in dealing with current crises and preparing for future ones. I suggest that you make notes in this book after each chapter to add in lessons from your personal experience. Then you can apply these lessons to your organization and share them with others at work in order to gain alignment about the actions your organization needs to take.

If you come through this crisis a winner, clearly focused on your True North, you'll find that the confidence you gain to withstand any level of difficulty will enable you to be a far better leader, in good times and in bad.

Let's start the seven lessons by examining why it is so hard for leaders to acknowledge that they're in a crisis.

LESSON #1

FACE REALITY, STARTING WITH YOURSELF

It didn't take long to encounter my first big crisis in business. As a twenty-seven year old going into my first line assignment, I was packing my bags and moving to Minneapolis to become assistant general manager of Litton Industries' microwave oven business, when the news came over the radio. "The Surgeon General has just declared that microwave ovens may be hazardous to your health," the announcer said.

The next morning I arrived at my new office to find chaos and fear wreaking havoc with people in the fledgling organization, just as its first consumer products were being launched. We had only one product: the microwave oven. If the Food and Drug Administration (FDA) pulled it from the market, we were out of business. This event became the ultimate test for a young organization already suffering from weak leadership and a lack of confidence.

A week later, the corporation's executive vice president arrived on the scene. He arbitrarily directed us to recall the first one thousand products shipped, much to the dismay of our customers. My first instinct was to challenge him because we thought the products were safe.

He was correct, of course. He may not have had all the facts, but he had the wisdom to take the more conservative course. His decision may have saved the business. It forced us to recognize that our designs were not robust enough to meet the pending FDA standards. Nor did we have the disciplined quality control procedures to produce consistent products.

Before I moved to Minneapolis, my bosses and I thought responsibility for these shortcomings belonged with the head of operations. After being inside the organization for just a few days, I recognized that the real problem was the general manager's lack of leadership. He was frozen in place by constant conflicts within the organization and his own inexperience.

Instinctively, I jumped into the breach and brought my new direct reports together to face the reality that we had serious problems. We committed to work together until the problems were solved.

It didn't happen overnight.

As we struggled to meet the emerging federal standards for microwave emissions, I learned just how tough a crisis can be. Several nights I went into our factory at 3:00 A.M. to work with the engineers and quality experts to determine whether we could start the production line the next morning. After nine months of wrestling with the problems that ensued, I said out of exasperation, "In business school, I never realized it was this hard to make money."

The lessons from this experience have stayed with me throughout my career and were especially useful years later at Medtronic. I found out the hard way how important it is to get to the bottom of a problem rather than fixing it on the fly. I also recognized how easy it is to underestimate its consequences, especially when you're receiving so much negative publicity.

I learned firsthand the importance of understanding the mind-set of regulators and government officials and building a cooperative, problem-solving relationship with them instead of being defensive. I realized as well that in a crisis, you have to set aside your near-term profit plans and get the problems fixed, no matter how high the cost. Most important of all, I learned not to judge leadership from the outside before understanding what is going on internally.

FACING REALITY

In *Leadership Is an Art*, Max DePree writes, "The leader's first job is to define reality. The last is to say thank you." Before you can lead your organization through a crisis, you have to acknowledge that you are indeed in one. Next, you have to get everyone else to acknowledge it as well. Only then can you define the problems accurately and develop plans to deal with them.

Why is this so difficult? Leaders often go into denial about the urgency and severity of the challenges they are facing. Or they tend to blame external events, people, or organizations for their problems. Without accepting that the problem is theirs to fix, they cannot understand what they are dealing with.

Often the hardest part is to acknowledge your role in the origins of the crisis. Even when leaders acknowledge their responsibility, they may face significant resistance from their organizations in solving it because people have great difficulty in admitting their mistakes. This is why crises require so much skill on the leader's part.

Philip McCrea learned the hard way how difficult it is for a young entrepreneur to face reality in his fledgling business. Founding San Francisco–based Vitesse Learning in 2001 at age thirty-two, McCrea saw only upward possibilities for his Web-based sales training company. McCrea was highly skilled in bringing in contracts, which often contained significant amounts of custom software for his young software team to develop.

Starting with only $1.2 million of capital, Vitesse made money its first two years. When it missed its 2003 targets by 40 percent, McCrea was forced to raise an additional $500,000. Vitesse rebounded strongly in 2004, thanks to expanded agreements McCrea negotiated with numerous divisions of Johnson & Johnson, as well as moving into financial services and a custom contract with Corning.

McCrea was a born optimist whose entire life had been successful. He noted, "I sometimes get too aggressive about the results we will achieve. It has been a challenge for me to open up and see that I don't have all the answers."

In 2005 McCrea's business turned down once again, shortly after he moved his family to New Jersey to be closer to his customers. With software programmers left behind without clear leadership, software costs escalated, leading to a new cash flow shortfall. McCrea hesitated in addressing the core problem of leadership in his software group. Strapped for cash, he instead searched for external options and decided to sell Vitesse to a Canadian company with a software team in Nova Scotia.

The merger did not go well, as attempts to migrate software development to Nova Scotia led to sharp reductions in quality and extensive customer complaints. Eight months into the merger, McCrea resigned, feeling the business had no future. Six months later, the Canadians declared bankruptcy and shut down the company, and 175 people lost their jobs.

McCrea described the previous two years as an "emotional rollercoaster." For the first time in his life, he had to acknowledge he had failed. "I had to look myself in the mirror and accept my failure," he said. "My greatest growth came through learning that failure is okay. During this time I was intolerable. Although I wouldn't admit it, I was depressed and got angry very easily."

After reflecting on what went wrong, McCrea became CEO of ClearPoint Learning, a sales training software firm with low-cost operations in India. Having learned from his mistakes at Vitesse and how important it is to face reality, he felt well positioned for success at ClearPoint.

It isn't just entrepreneurs who struggle with facing reality. Veteran leaders have an equal amount of difficulty. In 1991 Salomon Brothers faced possible criminal prosecution for submitting false bids to the U.S. Treasury, but its management was in complete denial about what had happened. This caused its largest shareholder, Warren Buffett, to take control of the company. Buffett's first task was to get the organization to face reality. He immediately forced top management to resign, although its leaders were denying any knowledge of the false bids. Then he went against the advice of the company's lawyers and public relations specialists and agreed to provide complete transparency to the U.S. government, even if the information could be used against the company in a criminal prosecution.

Buffett understood the company would almost certainly face criminal indictments if it continued to stonewall investigations by the U.S. Treasury and Justice departments. That would have precluded Salomon from bidding in government auctions and put the company into bankruptcy. By putting his personal credibility on the line, Buffett spared Salomon from criminal indictments and was able to restore its operations. Salomon shareholders were fortunate that Buffett was so willing to step into this messy situation and keep the firm from going under.

That's what courageous leaders do when faced with a crisis.

DE-NIAL IS NOT A RIVER IN EGYPT

An example of organizational denial can be found in the difficulties pharmaceutical maker Merck had with its $2.5 billion pain-relief drug, Vioxx. After an intense battle with Merck over indications of cardiovascular effects from the drug, the FDA approved Vioxx for general marketing in 1999. As large numbers of patients began using the drug and additional studies were completed, concerns continued to arise about Vioxx's safety for cardiovascular patients.

Skeptical because the concerns were based on nonrandomized data, Merck executives decided to conduct a three-year randomized trial of high-risk cardiovascular patients while continuing to market the drug. In September 2004, Merck halted the study at the midway point because results showed Vioxx patients were twice as likely to suffer a heart attack or stroke as those on placebo. Merck CEO Ray Gilmartin courageously pulled the drug from the worldwide market for all users, not just those at high risk of cardiovascular disease.

By then Vioxx was linked to more than twenty-seven thousand heart attacks and sudden cardiac deaths and a rising flood of lawsuits from plaintiff's attorneys. Merck wisely chose to defend Vioxx on a case-by-case basis, which may have saved the company from insolvency. After three years of fighting the attorneys to a draw, Merck announced a $5 billion settlement with the plaintiffs in 2007. The company had finally put its agony behind it.

Why did Merck, a company known for its scientific prowess, not take the more conservative course of restricting access to Vioxx? From the outside, it appears that Merck was so committed to using Vioxx to compete in the pain-relief market with Celebrex and other painkillers that it waited until proof was in from its own scientific study. When the study confirmed the problem, management immediately took action. By then, the damage was done.

WHY IT'S SO HARD
TO FACE REALITY

Denying reality has destroyed more careers and organizations than incompetence ever did. Instead of asking yourself why it is so difficult for other leaders to face reality, ask yourself instead, "Why is it so hard for *me*?"

The first reason is that people always prefer good news or a quick fix. Rarely are they willing to acknowledge that their organization is facing a crisis. Crises often start out in relatively benign ways, and then seemingly minor events escalate into major ones. Unless leaders face reality early, they can easily miss the signals of the deeper crisis that is waiting ahead. Until its leaders acknowledge the crisis, their organizations cannot address the difficulties.

Many people find reality is just too horrible to face or they are too ashamed, so denial becomes a convenient defense mechanism. If you feel yourself getting defensive, ask yourself, "What am I defending against? How might denying reality make the situation worse?"

DON'T SHOOT THE MESSENGER

In January 2009 I was chairing a panel on "Crisis, Community, and Leadership" in Davos, Switzerland, when panelist Jamie Dimon, J. P. Morgan's CEO, shared this vignette: "At a management meeting a woman got up and said, 'If you're a leader, you need one person who tells you the truth every time something goes on.'" To which Dimon noted, "If you have ten people around you and only one of them is telling you the truth, you have a real problem, because everyone has to do it."

Why aren't there more truth tellers in organizations? The reason is that they are afraid of getting in trouble with a boss who won't accept bad news. Leaders who are approached by a bearer of bad news may wind up shooting the messenger, because reality is just too painful to face. Look at what happened to Enron's Sherron Watkins when she took her concerns about financial misstatements to chairman Ken Lay. She was not only rebuffed but ostracized within the firm. No wonder many employees hesitate to tell the truth to their bosses.

Sadly, most organizations operate more like Enron than J. P. Morgan. Instead of building an organization of truth tellers, many leaders surround themselves with sycophants who tell them only what they want to hear, rather than sharing the stark reality. Without a culture of openness and candor, leaders are highly vulnerable to missing the signals of big problems ahead. By the time they acknowledge how deep their problems are—or outsiders like government agencies, consumer watchdog groups, or the media do it for them—it is too late. Then they find themselves forced to defend their companies against charges that are even worse than reality.

I used to tell people at Medtronic, "You'll never get fired for having a problem, but you will get fired for covering one up. Integrity is not the absence of lying. Rather, it is telling the whole truth, so that we can gather together the best people in the company to solve the problem."

It is important to publicly express appreciation to the truth tellers so others in your organization will follow suit. Only with a culture of candor and openness can organizations cope with crises and act in unison to get on top of them.

IT'S HARD TO ADMIT YOUR MISTAKES . . .

As a young civilian in the Office of Secretary of Defense Robert McNamara in 1966, I saw firsthand the consequences of an organization where people could not admit their mistakes. In the early years of the Vietnam War, McNamara was in complete denial about the war's progress. He used his intellect to intimidate the military and civilians to produce quantitative analyses showing the United States was winning.

Given his quantitative proclivities, McNamara saw Vietnam as a war of attrition. To measure progress, he tracked the ratio of enemy troops killed to American troops killed, under the assumption that the North Vietnamese and Vietcong would eventually run out of guerrilla fighters if enough were killed.

Since we knew the number of American troops lost, and the figure was rising rapidly, the only way to improve the ratio was to increase the number of enemies killed. This led to a systemic overstating of the number of North Vietnamese and Vietcong killed. My college ROTC buddies were telling me that dead bodies of enemy troops were counted three and four times by different units, just to improve their kill ratios.

To verify the data, my boss, the Pentagon's chief financial officer, forced the military intelligence community to remove the numbers of estimated enemies killed from their force strength. In the eleven months leading up to the Tet offensive in January 1968, official reports showed that the numbers of Vietcong had dropped precipitously. After inflated reports that thirty to forty thousand enemy troops died during Tet, the report's fallacies were exposed, and the report was never published again.

What I saw up close in Secretary McNamara was a leader in agony. He knew intuitively that the war was not going well but was unwilling to admit it. This resulted in those around him providing misleading information. The Pentagon never acknowledged that the United States was losing the war, and tens of thousands of brave American soldiers gave their lives for a poorly defined goal. In his acclaimed documentary, *The Fog of War*, producer Errol Morris captured McNamara in his sunset years, a man tormented by what went wrong but still unable to admit his mistakes.

Sound familiar? In 2003 Vice President Richard Cheney used similar tactics to generate data about the threat in Iraq from weapons of mass destruction, including false information about uranium supplied to Iraq by Nigeria. As British philosopher Edmund Burke said, "Those who don't know history are destined to repeat it."

. . . UNTIL YOU ACKNOWLEDGE YOUR ROLE IN THE PROBLEMS

In 2007 Amgen, the world's largest biotechnology company, faced growing safety concerns over Aranesp, its highly successful anemia drug with $4 billion in annual sales. After six years on the market, a series of studies conducted by Amgen, Johnson & Johnson, and others revealed problems with off-label use of Aranesp.

To deal with the growing crisis, CEO Kevin Sharer tasked his key executives with developing a plan to address the problems. But he found they wouldn't move until he acknowledged his own role in the crisis. "For a deeply reflective hour, I asked myself what I owned of this problem. I came up with a long list," said Sharer.

When he met with the executives to go over his list, they were stunned that their CEO would admit his errors. This freed them up to address their roles in the crisis and take necessary actions to get out of it. Well aware of the Merck experience with Vioxx, Amgen voluntarily agreed to more restrictive language on Aranesp package inserts. As a result, sales dropped by 26 percent, or more than $1 billion, but the company recovered. Aranesp is still on the market, albeit with a reduced patient population, and Amgen's relationship with the FDA is healthy once again.

Reflecting on what he learned from this crisis, Sharer noted, "The toughest thing was to embrace the reality that we had to take action because so many stakeholders had questions about the safety of Aranesp."

> *Our first reaction was to blame these problems on the FDA. We had to get above the fray and recognize that public health officials had legitimate questions about what was happening. First, I had to acknowledge my role in the crisis. Then we could face reality together by owning the problem and looking realistically at the decisions we had made.*

Sharer stresses the importance of being adaptive to new realities in a crisis. He notes that many CEOs fail to adapt because they get stuck in a comfortable mind-set with their version of reality. He cites his favorite analogy from biology: "What species survives? The biggest? The strongest? The fastest? No, it's the most adaptive."

> *In today's world, the penalty for non-adaptive behavior is severe. With the velocity of information on the internet, reaction times must be much shorter as the failure to adapt will be quickly noticed, amplified, and punished.*

Far too few leaders are willing to accept responsibility for their mistakes. Instead, many ignore problems and hope they go away. But like tumors growing inside the body, problems left unaddressed only get worse. If you face a similar situation, ask yourself, "What's the worst that could happen?" Whatever your answer, it is not nearly as bad as compounding your errors by denying the problems.

LESSON LEARNED

The crisis isn't going to fix itself, so denying its existence can only make things worse—much worse. That reality must start with you and your acknowledgment of your role in the crisis itself. Then you have to guide your organization to face reality as well. As we will see in the next chapter, you cannot do it by yourself, so don't try to carry the problems on your shoulders alone.

LESSON #2

DON'T BE ATLAS; GET THE WORLD OFF YOUR SHOULDERS

D o you ever feel like Atlas—that you're carrying the weight of the world on your shoulders? That the whole organization is depending on you and you're not sure you can pull it off? And if you don't, everything you have built for years will collapse overnight?

I've had that precise feeling many times in my career, especially as CEO of Medtronic. Frequently I felt that resolving serious problems depended on my ability to lead the organization. If I made the wrong judgment, I feared the whole place might come tumbling down, and I would be responsible for the company's demise. No doubt my free-floating anxieties were overstated, but most of us have a fear-of-failure narrative going through our minds, along with our striving-for-success narrative.

When I felt like that, I knew it was time to step back, take a deep breath, and recognize that I was not in this situation alone. It was time to get the world off my shoulders and ask others for help. This meant turning to my teammates within the organization and people in my personal world who support me.

THE DANGERS OF TURNING INWARD

Faced with a pending crisis, some leaders take the whole burden on themselves. They retire to their offices to ruminate about the problems and try to work out solutions in their heads. People in the organization start speculating about what is happening with their boss, who seems so withdrawn. Then the rumors start, and they are always worse than reality.

That's what happened to former Morgan Stanley CEO Philip Purcell in 2004 when his firm was facing myriad problems. Instead of going out to the trading floors and talking to the traders to see what was happening or meeting with executives to devise solutions, Purcell often hunkered down in his office and kept to himself.

Eventually his denial was so palpable that a group of former executives turned against him and led a successful effort to force his loyal board to oust him. When John Mack took over the following year, he rebuilt the executive team and the firm's confidence. This enabled Morgan Stanley to come through the global economic meltdown in reasonable shape.

Sensing trouble internally, other leaders turn to the outside world to seek positive reinforcement. When former Hewlett-

Packard CEO Carly Fiorina was under pressure from her board in 2005 to address the company's growing operational problems, she focused on her gift of giving passionate speeches. Rather than take their advice and focus on the company's internal difficulties, instead she delivered over one hundred speeches outside the company in her last year at the helm.

DUELING NARRATIVES

One of the reasons leaders turn inward is that they fear failure and loss of self-esteem. My Harvard colleague Nitin Nohria and I believe that all of us operate with two narratives about ourselves. Our positive narrative is that we are capable and doing worthwhile work. Our negative narrative causes us to fear that acknowledging our shortcomings could ultimately destroy us and our self-esteem. A crisis tends to accentuate the negative narrative, and we retreat inward.

Since my teenage years, I have had both positive and negative narratives racing through my mind. The positive is my vision of success, and the negative is my fear of rejection. Outwardly I exude the vision of success that I can accomplish anything I focus my mind and heart on doing, but that fear of being rejected is still lurking in the dark recesses of my mind.

I never feared failing in business because I learned from my father that failure is normal. The question is not whether you will fail—we all fail at one point or another—but how you respond to failure. Are you able to pick yourself up, and learn from failure to ensure success next time around? That's what Phil McCrea did after leaving Vitesse Learning.

I was fortunate to be able to separate challenges I faced from my self-esteem rather than taking them personally. Even in the worst of times, I was confident that I was a capable leader who could rebound from the most difficult circumstances.

However, many successful leaders do take failure personally. Their image is so dependent on outward signs of success that they cannot separate professional success from their self-image. Failure may inflict such deep wounds on their self-esteem that they are never able to overcome these wounds, and so they live in a world of denial.

Rejection by my peers has been my great fear. In junior high and high school, I felt rejected by the in-crowd as not being cool enough. This was my problem, as my need to be accepted and recognized got in the way of building genuine relationships. Until I confronted these fears, I could not move forward with my positive vision. When I faced up to them, I found they dissipated, enabling me to focus my energy on realizing success.

 What are the competing narratives you wrestle with? Do your fears stand in the way of realizing your vision? Do they cause you to turn inward instead of reaching out to others for help? If you embrace your fears instead of running from them, they will gradually dissolve. One of the best ways to do this is to turn to your teammates and the important people in your personal world for help and support.

TURNING TO YOUR
TEAM FOR HELP

After twenty-nine years in merchandising at Target, Gregg Steinhafel became CEO in May 2008, succeeding Bob Ulrich, his longtime colleague and mentor. Ulrich was concluding fourteen remarkable years as CEO, a time when Target's stock rose ten times, from $5.48 to $54.00 per share. Serving on the Target board for twelve of those years, I watched with admiration as Target emerged as the leading competitor to Wal-Mart and one of the most creative retailers.

When Steinhafel took over, warning signs were on the horizon. After forty-four months of besting Wal-Mart in comparable store sales, Target fell behind the Bentonville giant just as economic storm clouds were gathering.

More worrisome was pressure from activist investor William Ackman. In spring 2007 Ackman acquired 8 percent of Target stock as the price was climbing to its all-time high. He immediately began pressuring Target to spin off its credit card business as retailers Sears and K-Mart had done.

The week Steinhafel became CEO, Target announced the sale of 47 percent of its credit card business to J. P. Morgan for $3.6 billion. As economic conditions worsened, Ackman urged Target to divest its real estate into a real estate investment trust.

Steinhafel immediately sought help from his staff and directors, including Ulrich. He enlisted outside advisors Goldman Sachs and legal counsel Wachtell Lipton. Working closely as a team, they concluded that Ackman's proposal could put the firm in jeopardy just as the U.S. economy was going into free-fall. Not only would Target lose control of its real estate, expenses would rise by $1.4 billion with continuing cost escalations, thereby diminishing its ability to compete with Wal-Mart. With the unanimous support of the board, Steinhafel rejected Ackman's proposals.

Steinhafel's challenges didn't end there. Frustrated by continuing losses in his Target portfolio—one of his leveraged funds declined 90 percent—and the board's rejection of his proposals, Ackman launched a proxy fight to replace five members of the Target board with his own slate.

Steinhafel had not expected he would be engaged in an all-out proxy fight to retain control over such a highly successful company. He knew he shouldn't carry this burden alone, so he sought the counsel and engagement of the best experts he could enlist. Thanks to the hard work of his management and his board, Steinhafel and his team won the proxy contest, garnering over 70 percent of shareholders' votes.

In watching Steinhafel during this intense crisis, I observed the importance of his wisdom and leadership in seeking help, while maintaining his composure. Unless they seek help to resolve problems, leaders take on an impossible load. This is why leadership can be so lonely. On our own, we are vulnerable to misjudging the problem. To get through severe crises, you need the full support of your teammates, as Gregg Steinhafel had.

Faced with an even worse set of circumstances in 2000, Anne Mulcahy took the helm of Xerox with the firm facing bankruptcy. Having spent her career in sales and marketing, Mulcahy knew she lacked financial expertise, so she turned to the experts, including an assistant treasurer, to educate her about balance sheet management.

Mulcahy was dedicated not only to saving Xerox but restoring it to greatness. She met individually with the company's one hundred top executives and asked if they would stay with the company despite the challenges ahead. The first two executives who ran major operating units said they preferred to leave. Nearly all the remaining ninety-eight agreed to join her on the difficult journey. Mulcahy's team became incredibly loyal to her in restoring Xerox, and she no longer felt alone.

In asking others for help, Steinhafel and Mulcahy overcame the loneliness of leadership and gained both insights and support.

LOOKING TO YOUR EXTERNAL TEAM

To avoid the pitfalls of carrying the world on your shoulders, you also need support from people outside the company to get through it. Your external support team cares about you personally and is far less inclined to judge your actions in the company. Although they lack detailed facts, people you know well can provide insights and advice you don't get from insiders.

By the time you are facing a crisis, it is too late to form your support team. The time to do so is when things are going smoothly. These people can then know you well, and you feel confident you can count on them when the going gets rough.

Your support team starts with having one person in your life with whom you can be completely open, honest, and vulnerable. For me, that person is my wife, Penny, who is always there to pick me up when I am down and willing to point out when I get off track. For you, that person might be your spouse, mentor, or best friend.

This person cannot help you if you share only parts of your story or protect your vulnerabilities. By knowing you intimately, he or she can help you discover your blind spots or point out what you are overlooking. If you don't have anyone in your life with whom you can be completely open, I suggest consulting with a professional counselor or therapist.

Having mentors is another tremendous asset. These days when I need advice and counsel, I turn to mentors like Warren Bennis, David Gergen, and Nitin Nohria. In addition, I have a support group of eight men that has been meeting weekly since 1975. We talk about our beliefs and issues in our personal lives.

In 1983 Penny and I organized a couples' group of eight that meets monthly and travels together around the world. During the difficult times I have faced at work and in my personal life, these people have always been there for me with wise counsel and loving support, and I have tried to be there for them as well.

When Penny was diagnosed with breast cancer in 1996, initially I wouldn't consider the possibility that her illness could ultimately be fatal, although she was very concerned. So I discussed her situation with my men's group, which pointed out I was in denial, quite possibly because I had lost my mother and my fiancée to cancer nearly thirty years before. After that, Penny and I were able to share our fears and recognize that we were not in this alone. With the grace of God, Penny made a complete recovery from cancer and has used the experience to transform her life.

BE WILLING TO BE VULNERABLE

One of the hardest things for leaders is being vulnerable with other people. It is also one of the most powerful. Exerting power over others through direct commands while appearing invulnerable is not at all motivating. When you open yourself up to others and share your fears and shortcomings, you connect with them at a deeper level. Exposing your vulnerabilities is an open invitation for others to share openly with you. In the process, you gain a higher level of support and commitment from people as well as their respect.

John Hope Bryant, who lived as a homeless person early in his life, is the founder of Operation HOPE. He has raised

$500 million to focus on financial literacy for the poor and serves as vice chair of the President's Council on Financial Literacy. In *Love Leadership*, Bryant writes, "Vulnerability is power." He continues,

> *Admitting weaknesses and owning up to mistakes have counterintuitive benefits. When you are honest, people are more likely to forgive you any weaknesses and mistakes. You are also able to make a stronger connection with others. That ultimately gives you an ability to persuade and influence people, which in turn strengthens your ability to lead.*

In the mid-1990s, Piper Jaffrey CEO Tad Piper faced the possible bankruptcy of his firm after a rogue trader's misdeeds led to a flood of lawsuits from disgruntled investors. For years, his firm had produced outstanding results until the market turned and the funds lost one-quarter of their value. As a number of suits came from investors Piper had known for many years, he was uncertain just whom he could trust.

At first, Piper vowed not to settle with the plaintiffs' attorneys. He was angered by a *Wall Street Journal* article suggesting the lawsuits could bury the firm because they were two to three times the firm's capitalization. Over a critical holiday period, he left his family on vacation to return home and figure out how to solve the growing problem. But things only seemed to get worse.

At the point of desperation, he had a long conversation with his wife. "I was lying in bed that night, thinking there's no good solution, until this bolt of lightning hit me," Piper said. Having gone through chemical dependency treatment three years before, he remembered the second step of Alcoholics Anonymous: "Believe that a power greater than ourselves could restore us." He resolved to do just that, saying he felt "an incredible sense of relief."

> *I knew I was not alone. It is lonely at the top, particularly when you get into a big-ass problem and you need help. I was also fortunate to have a fantastic spouse and a handful of really good friends that were there for me in spite of this problem.*

With renewed confidence, Piper decided to settle the lawsuits. But he didn't stop there. With his wife at his side, he met with the leaders of his branch offices and shared his fears with them. "I decided to be completely honest and totally vulnerable," he said.

> *I talked about my chemical dependency and my faith, and told them we were moving forward, helping each other, and using our friends. This was the most powerful thing we've ever done at the company. People have never forgotten it because I showed my vulnerability. All of a sudden everybody was on our team, even the skeptics. I would never have done that if I hadn't found myself in the middle of this crisis.*

Learning how to express your vulnerabilities on appropriate occasions is an emerging leadership skill. It needs to be used with care, so that people can have confidence in your leadership and the direction you are leading them.

BUILDING YOUR RESILIENCE

The pressures on the leader that a crisis brings can be enormous. Crises often hit when you least expect them, so you need to be prepared. As crises drag on, you start wondering, "When will this ever end?" The truth is that no one knows.

To perform at your best throughout the crisis, you need a high level of resilience: a combination of hardiness, toughness, and buoyancy of spirit. These are challenging qualities to maintain during the rigors of a crisis, but they will sustain you through difficult times. That's why you need to build your resilience before the crisis hits.

Amgen's Kevin Sharer stressed just how important his preparation was in guiding his leadership team through the Aranesp problems. "You must be resilient, both organizationally and personally, and be prepared to take punches from everywhere," noted Sharer. "Being resilient helps you avoid denial, adapt to constantly changing circumstances, and communicate effectively, both inside and outside the company."

Starting with my first crisis at age twenty-seven, I always felt I was in a pressure cooker right up to my last day at Medtronic. To cope, I developed a set of practices over the years to maintain my resilience. In sharing these with you, I

BUILDING YOUR RESILIENCE

1. Keep your body in shape.
2. Keep your mind sharp and spirits high.
3. Don't take yourself too seriously.

am not suggesting these practices are right for you or for others. You have to develop your own techniques. The important thing is to have a set of practices that you make habitual:

- **Keeping my body in shape.** Regular workouts at least three or four times per week are essential for me. I like to jog for twenty to thirty minutes, which builds physical resilience and helps me clear my head. I engage regularly in longer, more vigorous activities, such as skiing, playing tennis, riding, hiking, and climbing.

- **Keeping my mind sharp and spirits high.** Thirty years ago, Penny convinced me to attend a meditation course with her. As a result, I developed a meditation practice — twenty minutes, twice a day — that has been invaluable in getting through high-stress periods and coping with jet lag on frequent overseas trips. Meditation offers a sense of harmony and well-being that is essential for coping with the rigors of high-pressure situations. I also pray regularly and find time for personal reflection.

43

- **Not taking myself too seriously.** This is probably my biggest challenge, as I tend to be serious and focused. The things that work to loosen me up a bit (and it would be misleading to say I get completely loosened up) include deep conversations, laughter, a good movie or play, dancing, and relaxing with friends.

LESSON LEARNED

You cannot get through a crisis alone, so don't try. The good news is that you are not alone. People inside your organization and in your personal circle are more than willing to help you if you ask them and are willing to open up to them.

You will be much more effective in getting through a crisis when you get the world off your shoulders and share your burdens with others. With the team solidly supporting you, you are prepared to bring them together to dig deep for the root cause of the crisis and get the problems fixed once and for all.

LESSON #3

DIG DEEP FOR
THE ROOT CAUSE

In the early stages of a crisis, it is easy to mistake the first symptoms that appear for the real problems. It is human nature to attempt to fix the symptoms before the root cause is determined. Like the weeds in your backyard, crises have roots with long tentacles that are buried deep underground. If you cut down the weeds without removing the whole root, they will surely grow back.

As a leader, your natural instinct is to challenge bearers of bad news about whether things can really be that bad, or whether they are just doom-and-gloom people. You're inclined to jump in and get the problems fixed to make them go away. And therein lies the danger.

If you move too fast to devise solutions, you may underestimate the depth of the problem or misjudge its root cause: the problem may be more serious than anyone appreciates. If you surround yourself only with positive people, your team may reinforce your natural instincts to solve the problem before it is fully understood. Thus, you cover over the wounds rather than undergo surgery, while letting the real problem fester. Or your quick fix may eradicate the symptoms of the problem while masking its root cause.

TRUST, BUT VERIFY

As a leader during a crisis, you should insist that people give you the whole story. Then always protect them from negative consequences when they do. This means maintaining close contact with people throughout your organization, not just your direct reports. The military motto of "trust, but verify" applies here. It is a good thing to trust the people you work with, but you should always verify information through your first-hand impressions in the marketplace or with people working in labs or on production lines. This means being in the marketplace and testing reality for yourself against what you hear from your team. Although marketplace inputs are anecdotal and unsystematic, they nevertheless give you firsthand understanding that enables you to challenge information coming through the hierarchy.

To understand what is happening in Macy's retail stores, CEO Terry Lundgren says, "I just pop into stores, call store managers on their cell phones, and tell them to come down. Then we walk through the floor. They have had no time to prepare the store. I learn as much as anything I do, because I'm seeing exactly what our customer is seeing."

Leaders who stay in their offices holding meetings and reading reports instead of gathering firsthand information never have the benefit of using all their senses—touch, smell, sound, sight, and hearing—that trigger their emotions and their intuition to recognize far more than their intellect does.

During my twelve years at Medtronic, I gowned up and witnessed nearly a thousand procedures in the operating rooms and clinics of hospitals around the world. For someone who knew little about the medical business, these experiences helped me understand the nature of the physician-patient relationship and how our products enabled physicians to help their patients heal. The experience of seeing our products not work as intended and the reaction of the physicians (one was so angry he threw a catheter covered in blood at me) lit a fire under me to ensure that our company produced only perfect products.

I also spent a great deal of time wandering through Medtronic' factories and labs. I found that employees, like physicians, were quite willing to tell me what the company needed to do to improve. The openness and transparency of the Medtronic culture put the company in a much better position to get to the bottom of problems.

GETTING TO THE BOTTOM OF THE PROBLEM

When I took over leadership of Honeywell's space and aviation sector in 1987, I found that the military avionics business had several fixed-price defense contracts whose costs were exceeding the maximum price. After a series of meetings with management, we determined we had $25 million in overruns that had to be recognized immediately in our financial statements.

When I shared the problems with the corporate CEO and chief financial officer, they decided to communicate the problem immediately to the company's shareholders. This led to several critical reports, downgrades of the stock, and negative media stories.

From the numerous experiences I had had in dealing with problems, I knew we had to keep analyzing the problems to see if we had reached the bottom. As it turned out, we weren't even close. It took three months to dig fully into all the losses from overruns on fixed price contracts. When we compiled them, the overruns totaled $450 million.

The Honeywell board of directors was outraged because it had been led to believe there were no problems in these contracts and any overruns could be recouped through change orders. That was not so in the new environment for defense contracting, and we had to absorb the losses.

Major shareholders were even more upset, questioning whether the CEO and top management knew what we were doing. At one especially intense meeting with three hundred shareholders, I defended the CEO by explaining how we got into this predicament and how we were going to get out of it. I prepared myself for the barrage of questions by telling myself, *I didn't create this mess. I'm just the guy sent in to clean it up.*

After months of meetings, I finally discovered the root cause of what had happened. Two years before, my predecessor had directed that no new estimates would be made of cost to completion on defense contracts in order to avoid losses being recognized. By not acknowledging a growing problem, management could not take corrective action, and the magnitude of the problem kept increasing.

Later I asked my boss how he thought I had handled the situation. He replied, "You did a good job of uncovering the problem and getting to the bottom of it, but you should have brought forward the entire $450 million problem at the outset." He was right, but at that early stage, no one had any idea how large the problem was. It took months, not days, to dig it out.

In retrospect, here's what I should have said at the start: "We uncovered $25 million in overruns we need to disclose now. We aren't sure if we're just looking at the tip of the iceberg, so we are continuing to investigate as the problems could be much deeper." That would have unsettled the stock market for a few months, but it would have avoided the credibility problem the company faced when it eventually disclosed the full magnitude of the losses.

Maintaining credibility trumps uncertainty every time.

DISCOVERING THE ROOT CAUSE

Medtronic had an agonizing experience with quality problems in the mid-1980s. Ten years earlier, defective batteries in the company's pacemakers had failed at an unacceptably high rate. The organization, which prided itself on healing patients with high-quality products, went into denial, unable to believe its products were harming patients. Although defective batteries were replaced with a newer design, the company never got to the root cause of why these failures occurred.

In 1984, the company had a similar experience when its pacemaker leads started failing. Again the organization went into denial. That led to a management change in which my predecessor, Win Wallin, took over as CEO and literally saved the company.

Wallin gathered key people together and insisted on two things: (1) an in-depth analysis of the root cause to ensure that these problems could never happen again and (2) complete transparency, inside and outside the organization, as a vehicle to force insiders to deal with the problems. The latter meant turning over internal data to government authorities and regulatory bodies in spite of the risks that the information could be used against the company.

As Wallin made people look at the pacemaker lead problem realistically, it became apparent that the real problem was the company's failure to examine the reasons for each returned product that failed to function properly. The engineers tended to deny a problem existed until failures exceeded certain statistical limits. Many product problems were never reported because hospitals did not always submit failure reports. By the time the problems were statistically significant, the impact was widespread. Key people inside the company became defensive as a result of the barrage of criticism from physicians, patients, and external consumer groups.

In response, Medtronic management decided to track down every report of a product problem to determine the extent to which the problem might be present in similar products. It also instituted a tracking system to monitor problems in leading hospitals and publish the cumulative data on a quarterly basis.

The key difference between Wallin and his predecessors was that he was a leader who demanded that the experts get to the root cause of the problems as quickly as possible. Leaders don't need to solve the problems themselves. Instead, they need to ask probing questions to ensure the real problem is identified and corrected. Otherwise the odds are high that superficial solutions will create other problems with unintended consequences.

When I joined Medtronic four years later, attitudes were very different. People talked openly about problems and vowed they would never occur again. This didn't mean the company could avoid product problems, as imperfections in implantable medical devices are inevitable. Even in 2008, Medtronic was still challenged by these issues in a case with a new defibrillator lead. However, the company's early warning systems enabled CEO Bill Hawkins to take immediate action to replace the product with an older, proven design.

Unless the root cause is corrected, the odds are high that the organization will find itself in yet another crisis in just a matter of years. It's your job as a leader to prevent that, or the next time around the situation will be a lot worse.

HAVE YOU FOUND THE ROOT CAUSE?

It isn't easy to determine whether you've gotten to the root cause. The only way to do so is to gather all your experts to analyze the problem and give them time to reach definitive conclusions. It is also helpful to engage outside experts to offer their perspectives.

At Medtronic we used physician customers who understood the clinical nature of the problems and scientists who understood the problems from a "first principles of science" viewpoint. When the problem was fully analyzed, corrective solutions could be determined. Solutions also must be confirmed by rigorous testing and internal and external experts. Even so, there was always uncertainty about whether the solution was correct.

When the problem is technologically challenging, this analysis takes time. When external pressure is mounting for answers, time is difficult to come by. Nevertheless, the alternative of offering an incorrect assessment is much worse. During this uncomfortable period, frequent updates to those concerned are required, along with reassurances that people are devoting their full-time attention to solving the problem.

When your organization is confident that it has developed corrective solutions, an intense effort is required to implement the solutions. As the leader, however, you should express cautious optimism, but not complete confidence, that you have an acceptable solution.

DÉJÀ VU: A CRISIS RETURNS

One of the most widely acclaimed examples of crisis management is Johnson & Johnson CEO Jim Burke's handling of the 1982 Tylenol crisis. In Chicago an unidentified person caused the death of two people by lacing capsules of Tylenol with cyanide poison. After a third person died in Los Angeles, Burke immediately ordered a nationwide recall of Tylenol from retail store shelves.

With J&J teams working around the clock to develop solutions, Burke became a familiar figure on the nightly news as his calming influence kept the panic from getting worse. Within six weeks, J&J had an alternative solution using tamper-evident packaging that enabled Tylenol to return to market and recapture its lost market share.

Burke justifiably became a national hero for his handling of the crisis. He said at the time that the packaging was not tamper proof, as such a design was not possible, but he also noted privately that if another event ever occurred, the brand was in trouble.

Less well known is the repeat event that occurred four years later when a young woman named Diane Elsroth died of poisoning from Tylenol capsules. To Burke, the news of the death brought on a nightmarish sense of déjà vu. "We didn't believe it could happen again," he said. Since this appeared to be an isolated incident, Burke hesitated to withdraw the Tylenol capsules from the market.

This time the media were unforgiving. At a press conference the day after the incident, Burke labeled the poisonings "an act of terrorism. Pure and simple." Burke also chastised the media for "turning this thing into a circus." He went on to tell them, "When you use words like *horror* and phrases like *national nightmare* over and over again, I think it is outrageous." Fortunately, J&J had an alternative pill design of caplets that was tamper proof. Under pressure, Burke decided six days later to replace all Tylenol capsules with the caplets, at an estimated cost of $150 million.

The next night Burke was asked on national news, "What would you tell the mother of Diane Elsroth?" Videos show Burke sweating and nervously scratching his head as he responded, "I would tell her I wish we had implemented this solution four years ago." His remarkably candid response calmed the national press and is characteristic of Burke's authenticity.

J&J's painful experience illustrates just how hard it is to get to the root cause. Burke's leadership enabled J&J to sustain its reputation for putting consumers first. Two decades later, Tylenol is still the leading painkiller on the market and J&J's reputation is intact.

BRINGING YOUR TEAM TOGETHER

After a dozen years of 18 percent annual growth, Medtronic sales slowed sharply in 1998. Having experienced our best years ever in 1996 and 1997, I was so accustomed to rapid growth that I thought this was a temporary slowdown. However, our business heads said that growth simply wasn't there. We were losing share in several markets to more competitive products and seeing a general slowdown in others.

Frustrated, I asked our financial people to analyze the underlying growth in each of our businesses. I didn't like the results. The analysis showed that market growth rates would not enable the company to sustain its 15 percent revenue growth, our public goal.

Gathering our executive committee together, I asked our chief financial officer to present the analysis and opened up the discussion. Several members felt the solution was to lower Medtronic's annual growth targets to 10 to 12 percent. Others suggested spinning off money-losing businesses and new ventures. One forcefully argued that the company should return to its roots in pacemakers and defibrillators. And the vice chair favored expanding through acquisitions.

Prior to this session, I thought the root cause was that Medtronic could not achieve its growth goals by focusing on existing markets. With marketplace growth slowing from 8 to 6 percent and Medtronic market shares in most businesses exceeding 50 percent, it was unrealistic to expect a 15 percent growth rate with our current business portfolio.

I saw two choices. One was to lower the growth goals to realistic levels, let the stock price seek its natural level, and abandon our ambitions of becoming the world's leading medical technology company. The second, and riskier, option entailed making acquisitions to enter higher-growth markets. My instincts were to pursue the latter course, but there were three problems with it: (1) the company's track record in integrating acquisitions had been uneven at best, (2) acquisitions would take time before they would have an impact on the bottom line and there was no assurance of getting them done, and (3) four of our top executives opposed this approach.

In the intense debates that followed, I realized that the fundamental issue was *not* slowing growth in Medtronic's markets. The deeper problem was that our organization was losing confidence in its ability to sustain growth, compounded by the fatigue of twelve years of consecutive growth.

Uncharacteristically, I decided to abandon achieving a consensus. Instead I took responsibility to pursue the acquisition route with a small team of senior people, while tasking the rest of the organization with restoring growth in current businesses by accelerating new products to market. I recognized this highly risky course was a make-or-break decision for my leadership that could easily backfire.

As it turned out, good fortune shone as the stars aligned just in time and attractive acquisition candidates became available. Medtronic made five major acquisitions in the space of six months, followed later by a sixth and then a seventh. These seven acquisitions were expensive, costing $14 billion, because they involved leading companies in high-growth markets. In the end, they transformed Medtronic from a pacemaker-defibrillator company into the world's leading medical technology company.

The process was messy and filled with disagreements, as such tough issues often are. In the end, conflict was required to get to a highly favorable outcome. There is no doubt we were lucky, but I never believed in luck as raining down like manna from heaven. Rather, I prefer Oprah Winfrey's definition of luck as "preparation meeting opportunity." As hockey great Wayne Gretzky once said, "You miss 100 percent of the shots you don't take."

LESSON LEARNED

An organization cannot deal with a crisis until it determines its root cause, but people are often mentally blocked from recognizing it because the implications are so frightening. The leader must bring people together to confront their worst fears and address the risks. In Medtronic's 1998 crisis I learned that my teammates were willing to commit to the aggressive course only when I was willing to take those risks on my shoulders. The hesitancy and fears of failure that many felt were then channeled into turning this risky decision into a major success.

In the following lesson, we examine how crises can drag on and why you as the leader need to get your organization prepared for an extended battle in order to emerge successfully at the other end.

LESSON #4

GET READY FOR
THE LONG HAUL

It is tempting to think of crises as events to weather until things return to normal. As hard as it is to predict when a crisis will hit, it is even more difficult to forecast when it will end.

There is great danger in prematurely declaring victory over a crisis. Look at the impact of President George W. Bush's landing on the deck of the aircraft carrier *Lincoln* in a green flight suit and declaring that the war in Iraq was over in front of a giant "Mission Accomplished" sign. Don't tell that to all those brave soldiers who have fought in Iraq the past six years. The lack of credibility of this event undermined support for the war, as well as for President Bush's leadership.

Even when an organization is in a full-fledged crisis mode, many people assume that they just need to make tactical changes to get through the crisis, like cutting back production schedules until demand comes back. It is just a matter of time, they argue, until the business returns to where it was in its heyday. Like sailors at sea, they batten down the hatches until the storm passes. But what if the storm goes on for a long time? What if fundamental changes in direction are required?

When facing a crisis, it is prudent for you to assume that the crisis will last a long time. When things return to "normal" (if there is any such thing as normal), everything will be different. When you sense a problem coming, ask yourself whether you are looking at a harmless piece of ice floating on the surface or the tip of the iceberg. If you don't know for sure, this isn't the time to move full speed ahead. If you do, you're asking for trouble.

THINGS WILL GET WORSE

When you find yourself getting into a crisis, it is human nature to think things couldn't get any worse. Trust me, things could get a lot worse. More often than not, the situation deteriorates before it gets better.

In the 2008–2009 economic crisis, many people ignored the early signals of the subprime mortgage crisis. Even the forced sale of Bear Stearns to J. P. Morgan did not send out sufficient alarms that other financial institutions could face similar fates. Only when Lehman Brothers, AIG, and Merrill Lynch blew up in the same week in September 2008 did financial leaders start to recognize how grave the situation had become.

In early 2007, Goldman Sachs's trading unit experienced a modest loss in subprime mortgages, including the impact of the bankruptcy of New Century Financial, a mortgage banker. With a $1.2 trillion balance sheet, this may not have seemed like such a major problem to a firm like Goldman.

As Goldman's top executives explored its position in subprime mortgages in considerable depth, they realized that this situation could become catastrophic if immediate action was not taken. They decided to get out of the subprime business and stop doing business (other than advisory) with firms like Countrywide Financial that specialized in subprime mortgages. Meanwhile, Countrywide, Citigroup, UBS, and AIG aggressively pursued subprime mortgages until everything collapsed eighteen months later.

In avoiding the bulk of the just-emerging subprime mortgage crisis, were the top managers at Goldman smarter than everyone else or just lucky? Probably neither. They were superb risk managers who analyzed every aspect of their highly complex business until they understood its risks and ramifications. By marking its holdings to market each day, Goldman recognized the subprime mortgage problem earlier than others and was able to limit the firm's exposure by getting out of the business a full year before others did.

Goldman's leadership avoided the trap of thinking things couldn't get worse. Instead, they kept digging into the problem with their specialists, and came to the realization that it could get a lot worse, as it did for so many other firms, if they didn't take corrective action immediately.

CRISES HAVE LONG ROOTS

Leaders often fail to see the crisis coming. Rather than acknowledging they should have recognized the signals in time, they blame external events and things outside their control. Many behave as if the crisis came out of nowhere or was an act of God, like Hurricane Katrina. Reality is usually very different. To quote Xerox CEO Anne Mulcahy when she visited my Harvard Business School class, "A lot of crises seem to happen overnight, but they have really long roots, like ten to fifteen years in terms of the source of the real problems."

As an example, let's examine the origins of the current problems at Citigroup, which date back to Sandy Weill's tenure as CEO. Weill's success made him a Wall Street icon with enormous power. Under his leadership, Citigroup had a dynamic, growth-oriented culture. What it lacked was sufficient board oversight or risk management. When Chuck Prince took over as CEO in 2003, he had to give top priority to resolving the myriad legal and ethical problems that Weill left behind. In Prince's first year, Citigroup paid over $5 billion in fines and legal settlements.

Evidently this was just the tip of the iceberg. The problems uncovered after Prince resigned in November 2007 forced Citigroup to obtain $351 billion in equity investments and loan guarantees from the U.S. government to keep from going under. In response, CEO Vikram Pandit announced layoffs of seventy-five thousand employees in late 2008.

In a similar vein, AIG's massive problems forced the U.S. Treasury to take 80 percent ownership in the company, appoint Ed Liddy as CEO, and provide $173 billion in bailout funds to keep the firm afloat. AIG's problems resulted from

the loose conglomerate of companies built by Liddy's predecessors, Hank Greenberg and Martin Sullivan.

Like Weill, Greenberg also had a powerful, heroic image.
He created the market for credit default swaps in 1987 and
dominated his firm and his board. In 2006 he was ousted following an accounting scandal. Greenberg is a tragic figure in
many ways: a successful builder who could not adapt to
twenty-first-century rules.

It is easy to categorize Weill, Greenberg, and their suc-
cessors as failed leaders, but that assessment may miss the nu-
ances of the situation. With unrelenting pressure from the
stock market to improve results, pulling back from the rollercoaster is extremely difficult. When markets are growing and
your firm is competing hard, it is easy to overlook signs of trouble and take even greater risks to keep profits flowing on the
assumption that markets will stay healthy.

TAKING DECISIVE ACTION

To combat this human tendency, the reflective qualities of
Intel CEO Andy Grove expressed in his book *Only the Paranoid Survive* are essential. By constantly fearing markets could
collapse tomorrow or his company's market leadership could
disappear overnight, Grove was ever alert to Intel's risks and
preparing his defenses if the worst occurred.

In 1984 Grove led Intel through its most challenging crisis: losing its position in the memory chip market to aggressive

Japanese competitors. Grove worked with his managers for an entire year to get costs down and stabilize prices, but nothing seemed to stem the tide of the relentless Japanese firms. They used their high-volume, low-cost position to price below Intel, leading to a sharp decline in Intel's market share. As its share plunged into single digits, Intel's red ink was flowing. Just as it seemed things couldn't get any worse for Intel, the bottom fell out of the memory chip market.

As Grove said, "Our order backlog evaporated like snow":

> We had meetings and more meetings, bickering and argu-
> ments, resulting in nothing but conflicting proposals. . . .
> As the debates raged, we just went on losing more and more
> money. It was a grim and frustrating year. We had lost our
> bearings. We were wandering in the valley of death.
>
> After this aimless wandering had been going on for
> almost a year, I was in my office with Intel's chairman and
> CEO, Gordon Moore, discussing our quandary. I asked,
> "If we got kicked out and the board brought in a new CEO,
> what do you think he would do?" Gordon answered with-
> out hesitation, "He would get us out of memories." I stared
> at him, numb, then said, "Why shouldn't you and I walk
> out the door, come back and do it ourselves?"

It wasn't easy. Grove spent another year convincing his team that the company had to get out of memory chips. As it did so, Intel shifted all its resources to microprocessors, where its technology offered a distinct competitive advantage.

This decision fueled Intel's success for the next two decades as its microprocessors became the heart of all personal computers and thousands of other devices. By continuing to drive its technology forward, Intel kept microprocessors from becoming a commodity—all because Grove recognized things could get worse and took decisive action.

Reflecting on why it is easier for outsiders to make decisions like this, Grove writes:

> People who have no emotional stake in a decision can see what needs to be done sooner. CEOs from the outside are no better managers or leaders than the people they are replacing. They have only one advantage, but it may be crucial: the new managers come unencumbered by such emotional involvement and therefore are capable of applying an impersonal logic to the situation. They can see things much more objectively than their predecessors did.

REINVENTING YOUR LEADERSHIP

Avon CEO Andrea Jung faced a similar situation when Avon's growth dropped sharply in 2005 after four years of rapid growth. In response, its stock price tumbled. A fellow CEO told her, "Pretend you were fired and got brought back in new."

Jung explained why this is so difficult. "The thing is, you're not new," she said:

You have to do it with all the relationships. You're taking out people you put in. They are not faceless names on an organization chart. If you can do it, it's the best of both worlds. You have the history, the passion, and the love of the place already. But you have to do some brutal things that some people cannot do when they get too inbred. It's harder emotionally and easier executionally because I know what rocks to look under.

Rather than taking a series of short-term actions, Jung decided to use the slowdown to transform Avon for the long term. First, she cut $300 million in expenses and reduced Avon's organizational layers from fifteen to eight. To take Avon in new directions, she decided to reinvest all of the savings in growth. When shareholders greeted her plans negatively and Avon stock declined further, Jung didn't flinch.

Entering 2006, Jung felt that she was a completely different leader than she had been in her first four years as CEO. "Being able to reinvent yourself personally as a leader is just as important as reinventing the company and its strategy," she reflected. Jung's gamble paid off as Avon's growth was restored, and two years later its stock reached a new high.

Facing such a decision yourself, are you prepared to walk out of your office, come back as "the new CEO," and make the most painful decision of your career, unencumbered by your emotional involvement but guided by an impersonal logic? If you are, you may become a great leader.

These stories of Goldman Sachs, Intel, and Avon as they faced crises all involve authentic leaders following their True

North by owning the problems they face. Their leaders had the wisdom to know the situation could get a lot worse. By probing the depths of the iceberg, they were able to scope out its magnitude and lead their organizations safely through the crisis. As a result, they put themselves in a stronger position coming out of the crisis.

IN A CRISIS, CASH IS KING

In a crisis, cash is king. Not earnings per share. Not revenue growth. Not return on equity. Survivability and fiscal conservatism must take precedence over near-term financial metrics. Ask yourself, do we have sufficient cash reserves to get through the worst crisis imaginable? If the answer is no, you should take immediate action to shore up your cash reserves.

The now widely held view that hoarding cash is bad and debt is good has been steadily evolving over the past twenty-five years. It started with the hostile raiders of the 1980s, who used Michael Milken's junk bonds and massive amounts of debt to take over companies, often against their will.

The Reagan era of low interest rates, easy availability of cash, and the emergence of creative financial vehicles and hedging tools changed the financial industry's view of cash. Investment banks showed their customers the advantages of leveraging their balance sheets by taking on large amounts of debt.

The stock market also shifted from valuing cash to devaluing it. As the stock market's focus became increasingly short term, cash was viewed as a drain on return on equity. Pressure mounted for cash-generating firms to buy back their stock to reduce cash balances. Small wonder so many financial institutions and companies found themselves cash starved when the global economic crisis hit with full force.

Wise leaders who are building their organizations need to resist these pressures and take a conservative course. As John Bogle, former CEO of Vanguard, says, "We have shifted from an 'ownership society' to an 'agency society.'" While the agents can sell your stock any time they choose, you have to run the company. If outsiders are pressuring you to leverage up your balance sheet, you will be wise to remember that your task as leader is to enable the organization to compete for the long term.

RESPONDING TO EARLY WARNING SIGNALS

There were early warning signals of the pending financial crisis in 2007. Goldman Sachs saw them in early 2007 with its analysis of subprime mortgages. In August that year, another shot came across the bow, as I was hiking with close friends in the Bugaboo Mountains of British Columbia. When I returned to the lodge around 5:30 P.M., Goldman Sachs CEO Lloyd Blankfein reached me and explained that quantitative funds, including three Goldman funds, had experienced a bad day in the market: with all sellers and no buyers, prices dropped sharply.

Concerned about the market's instability and growing systemic risks, Goldman's top executives decided to shift emphasis to building its global liquidity to weather a long economic storm. Meanwhile, Lehman Brothers continued to leverage its balance sheet for the next year while minimizing cash reserves. Lehman CEO Richard Fuld failed to acknowledge the storm clouds brewing in late 2007 and the first half of 2008. Even the collapse of Bear Stearns in March 2008 didn't cause Fuld to adjust his strategy.

On Sunday, September 14, 2008, Lehman was under such financial stress that it could not be saved before Asian markets opened. Merrill Lynch was hastily sold to Bank of America, and AIG was taken over by the U.S. government to avoid bankruptcy. This triggered a financial panic unlike anything else since the Great Depression.

Meanwhile, Goldman announced that its liquidity at the end of August 2008 exceeded $100 billion. It was a good thing, as liquidity pressures on all financial institutions spiraled upward. As credit markets froze and commercial paper dried up, investors withdrew their funds. As an insurance policy, Goldman arranged a $10 billion investment from Warren Buffett. His expression of confidence in the firm was worth even more than his money.

Yet financial storms didn't end there, as the crisis seemed to drag on interminably. Wachovia and Washington Mutual were forced into the hands of Wells Fargo and J. P. Morgan by the U.S. Treasury. Fourth-quarter results for 2008 hit disastrous levels, and financial institutions hung on for dear life. The financial crisis carved deeply into the U.S. economy and devastated national economies in Iceland and Ukraine.

Finally in April 2009, three firms that had assumed the worst about the economic devastation showed signs of recovery. Wells Fargo reported $3 billion in quarterly profits, and Goldman followed a few days later by reporting $1.7 billion profit, noting that global liquidity had grown to $164 billion. J. P. Morgan followed with $2.1 billion quarterly profit.

LESSON LEARNED

Many leaders will learn from the global economic crisis not to underestimate the length and severity of crises they face, even if their crises have nothing to do with the economy. When facing the early stages of a crisis, it is essential not to declare victory too soon. Prudent leaders recognize that survivability is their most important goal, so that they can come back strong as the crisis subsides.

In the next chapter, we explore leaders who see a crisis as an opportunity to achieve their goals.

LESSON #5

NEVER WASTE A GOOD CRISIS

In *The Prince*, Italian philosopher Nicolò Machiavelli advised his followers, "Never waste the opportunities offered by a good crisis." Although it is hard to recognize at the time, a crisis provides a unique opportunity to create transformative change in your organization.

When business is booming, staffing and spending levels inevitably expand too rapidly, and wasteful habits creep in. People become highly resistant to reductions in infrastructure and employment, arguing that cutbacks will hurt the company's growth and market position. In my years in business, I cannot think of a time when we cut too deeply or too soon. The greater danger lies in not recognizing the crisis early enough to take aggressive action. When that happens, revenues decline faster than expenses, and you never catch up.

HITTING THE WALL AT TEACH FOR AMERICA

As a twenty-two-year-old Princeton graduate, Wendy Kopp founded Teach For America (TFA) in 1989 with the vision of ensuring that every child had access to quality education. Her goal was to transform public education by creating a new corps of young teachers who would commit two years to educate inner-city children in grades K–12.

In 1995, after four years of initial success, TFA hit the wall. It was losing many of its early funders, applications to teach were declining, and a $2.75 million deficit loomed. To make matters worse, TFA was being attacked by the educational establishment as being bad for children. Working one hundred hours per week and facing overwhelming problems, Koop considered shutting down her fledgling organization or resigning to let someone else run it.

After a great deal of soul searching, Kopp decided to use the crisis to refocus TFA on its core mission. She reduced payroll 40 percent, shut down two strategic initiatives that were transforming education, and created the organization's first five-year plan.

As painful as these changes were, they led to the resurgence of TFA. By 2008 TFA's number of teachers had grown tenfold to sixty-six hundred, with 67 percent achieving "significant classroom gains." Even more important, TFA had twenty-two thousand alumni, 60 percent of whom stayed in education after their two-year stint with TFA.

For her leadership, Kopp was named one of America's Best Leaders and became a national spokesperson for education reform. Had it not been for Kopp's tenacity and her commitment to TFA's mission, the organization would never have survived the crisis. Instead, Kopp used the crisis as an opportunity to reposition TFA for sustainable success.

WASTING A GOOD CRISIS

In contrast to Kopp's leadership, the real tragedy occurs when management wastes a golden opportunity to transform itself. For three decades, General Motors management ignored the crises it faced, treating them as short-term events to get through rather than opportunities to transform the company. Frequently its executives turned to the U.S. government to help the company out of its predicaments, such as imposing import quotas on foreign-made vehicles, delaying federally mandated increases in fuel efficiency, or lobbying the government to take over its health care benefits.

GM management convinced the U.S. government in 1981 to reduce imports of Japanese-made vehicles to prevent Japanese manufacturers from increasing their U.S. market share. Instead of seizing on this golden opportunity to recapture share and invest in more competitive cars, GM used the reprieve to raise prices and restore flagging profit margins. When the import quotas were removed, GM was even less competitive with foreign-made vehicles.

77

In 1992 my wife and I entertained the head of GM's Cadillac division, who had come to Minneapolis for the NCAA Final Four Basketball Tournament. Knowing how sensitive GM executives were to riding in competitors' vehicles, I was embarrassed to pick him up in my Lexus, but we owned only foreign-made cars. At the time, Lexus, which had been on the U.S. market for two years, was rapidly taking market share from Cadillac.

To his credit, he immediately started quizzing me about what I liked about the Lexus. I proceeded to list a dozen things that were superior to any American auto I had ever owned. Then I asked him, "What do you think of it?" He responded, "I've never been in one." No wonder he and his colleagues compared their current automobiles to GM's previous models. Without management pressing its designers and marketers for objective comparisons to competitive products, it was easy to become self-referential.

GM always wanted to be the biggest in spite of its shrinking share of the market, which declined from 51 percent in the 1960s to 19 percent in 2009. During recessions, its management never cut deeply enough for fear of being caught short in the next upturn. In contrast, Ford constrained its spending and production to prepare for difficult times. When the automotive market collapsed in late 2008, it was too late for GM, and management was forced to turn to the U.S. government to bail the company out. The final straw occurred on June 1, 2009, when GM applied for Chapter 11 bankruptcy and turned 70 percent of its ownership over to the governments of the United States and Canada.

In 2006 Ford went outside automobile ranks to recruit Boeing's Alan Mulally as CEO. Three months after he joined the company, Mulally announced that Ford would mortgage all its assets for $23.6 billion in loans to finance an overhaul of the company. When Mulally said the loans would give Ford "a cushion to protect for a recession or other unexpected event," many observers considered this an act of desperation. In fact, Mulally's actions saved the company, avoiding the requirement for government bailouts and enabling Ford to operate as an independent company.

CREATING A CRISIS TO GET COMPETITIVE

Contrast GM's experience with the visionary leadership of Jack Welch. When he was elevated to CEO of General Electric in 1981, Welch saw a world ahead that few others recognized. He envisioned intense global competition in which only the leanest and most competitive firms would survive. Welch decreed that every GE business unit had to be number one or two in its industry and fully competitive, or GE would divest the business.

To get his slow-moving, mature organization to go along, Welch created a crisis. He shifted key positions to executives who agreed with his philosophy and retired the rest. There was no challenge he wasn't willing to take on. No detail was too small to escape his attention, and perhaps his wrath. He eliminated 100,000 jobs, including many layers of staff and line. In the process he turned GE's bureaucracy into a high-performance machine.

His aggressive style saddled him with the moniker "Neutron Jack." He offset this public image with intense focus on leadership development within GE. He turned Crotonville, New York, into the world's finest leadership development laboratory and went there regularly to engage in intense debates with midlevel executives.

Welch had two basic measures for his leaders: performance and values. One without the other was insufficient to get promoted. The performance metric was an obvious part of his strategy, but he made values equally important. Late in his tenure, he quite publicly terminated a high-ranking executive for not measuring up to GE standards for values, although the person had violated no laws. When Welch retired in 2001, GE was highly competitive and a major global player, largely due to the changes he made in anticipation of looming globalization of competition.

IN CONTRAST . . .

Welch's actions left rivals like Siemens, Philips, Westinghouse, and Mitsubishi wondering why they never could get their organizations to shed their bureaucracies. Although Siemens was considered the peer of GE in the 1970s, successive generations of executives could not get the company moving at GE's speed. As CEO from 1992 to 2005, Heinrich von Pierer made some progress in transforming Siemens, but the German giant still struggled to keep up with GE.

Replacing von Pierer in 2005, CEO Klaus Kleinfeld launched a major restructuring program and a crackdown on illegal conduct. Kleinfeld wanted to eliminate any inappropriate practices in the company, so he hired outside legal and auditing experts to revamp Siemens's internal accounting and control system.

In 2006 everything blew up for Siemens. An internal audit report revealed the company paid bribes totaling more than $3 billion. Chairman von Pierer denied responsibility, claiming he knew nothing about bribes paid while he was CEO. He defended himself by stating that each year he had sent statements to his managers reminding them of their responsibility to comply with the Siemens ethical code.

When it comes to business ethics, written statements are insufficient. Leaders have an obligation to get personally involved to ensure the company's ethical standards are upheld and verify the information through auditing business practices throughout the world.

By denying his culpability, von Pierer was unable to lead Siemens out of this crisis, and the Siemens board was forced to find new leadership. Kleinfeld also resigned to make way for a new executive team. Gerhard Cromme was selected as chair of the supervisory board, and Peter Loescher was recruited from Merck to become CEO.

Cromme had been head of Thyssen-Krupp for many years. Having served on nine different boards, he was highly respected as a governance expert. He settled charges emanating from the bribery scandals, completing negotiations with U.S. and European authorities in record time. Even so, the settlements cost Siemens $2.5 billion in fines and legal fees. Loescher immediately began the transformation of the company's management to make it leaner and more competitive.

The performance of General Electric and Siemens, both great companies, over the past twenty years provides a clear contrast in leadership effectiveness. Under von Pierer's leadership, Siemens operated in a traditional hierarchical style, whereas Welch turned GE upside down to make it fast moving, dynamic, and highly competitive. It took major scandals to shake Siemens up to recognize it needed a complete overhaul. GE and Siemens provide vivid examples of why leadership is so important, as do Ford and General Motors.

USING A CRISIS TO FUEL THE FUTURE

Medtronic faced a looming crisis in 1993, triggered by the proposed Clinton health care plan. We feared this plan would lead to mandated price reductions for our pacemakers, defibrillators, and other high-margin products. That would threaten our strategies of high R&D investment and extensive support for physicians during implant procedures.

In response, we made massive cuts in product costs, overheads, and infrastructure expenses. We also took advantage of the opportunity tó restructure and simplify our organization with fewer layers, meetings, and "nice-to-dos." But we were unwilling to abandon our strategies of heavy investments in R&D and physician support.

To gain organizational support for these massive changes, including a companywide pay freeze, Medtronic executives agreed to take pay cuts and give up their perquisites: company cars, club memberships, and financial counseling were eliminated, and a ban went into effect on reserved parking places, an executive dining room, and a company airplane. The important thing about abolishing the perquisites was not the cost savings, but reinforcing the egalitarian character of the Medtronic culture.

As it turned out, the much-feared price reductions never came to pass, but the massive cost reductions did. They led to increased profit margins, enabling Medtronic to go on the offense to gain market share. A portion of cost reductions was used to finance increases in R&D spending from 9 to 11 percent of sales, while reducing product development lead times from forty-eight to eighteen months. Several hundred specialists were added to support physicians during procedures.

These aggressive moves caught Medtronic's competitors off guard as its share of the pacemaker-defibrillator market grew from 40 to 50 percent. Meanwhile, high cash flow from this business ultimately funded Medtronic's expansion into other areas of medical technology and developing markets.

By shifting the focus of competition to R&D and product support, Medtronic played to its greatest strengths, making it difficult for Medtronic competitors to compete profitably. As a result, Siemens, Eli Lilly, Sanofi, Sulzer, and Pacific Dunlop spun off their medical device business.

This was one crisis we didn't waste. It laid the groundwork for fifteen more years of rapid growth and expansion.

LOU GERSTNER AND THE TRANSFORMATION OF IBM

Rarely has any major corporation come back from as severe a crisis as the one IBM faced in the 1990s. The world's leading computer company was suffering from competition from Microsoft and Intel's lower-cost microprocessor-based systems that ravaged IBM's profit margins and exposed its high cost structure.

A colleague who served on the IBM board at the time said he had never seen a business turn so quickly from solid profits to massive losses. Things were so bleak inside IBM that its strategic planners were giving serious consideration to breaking IBM's complex structure into thirteen pieces to spin off to prospective investors.

Board members recognized the depth of IBM's problems and its need for new leadership. They approached Lou Gerstner, who had just completed the transformation of R. J. Reynolds Tobacco, and convinced him to save an American treasure. Gerstner immediately set about revamping IBM from top to bottom. He forced its managers to face the reality of rapidly falling profits from aging mainframe computers and the need to rebuild its frayed customer relations, which had been the hallmark of the company.

To lead the massive cost cutting, Gerstner recruited Jerry York from Chrysler as his chief financial officer. York knew nothing about the computer business, but he knew how to cut costs. The proverbial "bad cop" with a job to do, York didn't care what people thought of him and was impervious to criticism. He also permitted Gerstner to play the role of "good cop," who focused on rebuilding IBM's customer relations.

Gerstner's brilliant strategic insights and leadership skills not only saved IBM from Joseph Schumpeter's "creative destruction," but restored its industry leadership and its shareholder value. For IBM, this was one crisis that was anything but wasted.

LESSON LEARNED

The leadership stories of GE's Welch and IBM's Gerstner are fulsome examples of how great leaders use a crisis to transform their enterprises. These examples don't apply just to major companies. They are equally effective in smaller and midsized organizations, where the need for restructuring and transformation is also great.

Leaders who don't take advantage of crises to make long-term changes not only waste their opportunities but sow the seeds for a repeat experience. Like General Motors, your organization will face these risks if you don't make the required changes.

Now let's turn to the question of how, as a leader, you can deal with being in the spotlight, both internally and externally, and still stay on track of your True North.

LESSON #6

YOU'RE IN
THE SPOTLIGHT:
FOLLOW TRUE NORTH

In today's world you don't have to be a politician or a celebrity to be a public figure. As a leader in business or a nonprofit, you are constantly in the public eye, whether you like it or not. Your compensation is published in the newspaper. Your statements are widely quoted. People inside and outside your organization speculate about what you are thinking.

The modern media world with its multiplicity of new information sources presents myriad pitfalls and opportunities. In a crisis, everything is amplified one hundredfold. The world of the Internet has democratized information and dramatically increased its velocity of transmission. As a leader, you need to find ways to use it to your benefit rather than bemoan its downsides.

No one did this more skillfully than President Barack Obama in his successful 2008 presidential campaign. As effective as his team was in sending consistent messages through every possible media vehicle, Obama was still plagued with guilt by association with the fiery sermons of his pastor, Reverend Jeremiah Wright, missteps by his economic advisor Austan Goolsbee, and offhand comments by supporter Samantha Power, who called Hillary Clinton "a monster."

When I joined high-profile conglomerate Litton Industries in 1969, its public relations specialist told me that chairman Charles "Tex" Thornton directed him to keep the company hidden in the tall grass. In response, he told him, "Tex, when you're standing ten feet tall, you can't hide in tall grass." The heads of today's leaders are way above the grass, so they might as well take advantage of the visibility rather than let it whipsaw them.

With the widespread use of blogs, Twitter, and YouTube, nearly anyone can get exposure as an instant media expert. The more extreme someone's views are, the more attention they seem to receive. Articles and video clips get passed on to friends of friends, and suddenly the whole world is watching. Plaintiffs, attorneys, and government regulators frequently subpoena massive numbers of company e-mails, sifting through them to find employee comments that will support their cases.

During a crisis, the spotlight on leaders is turned up to maximum intensity. People are so nervous and hungry for information that they hang on every word from their leaders, trying to glean clues from their body language, facial expressions, and even the color of their ties and dresses.

In the glare of the lights, your ability to stay true to your values is put to the test. You can make or break your reputation in an instant. Look at the leadership of New York City mayor Rudy Giuliani in the aftermath of the attacks of September 11. While national leaders retreated to their bunkers, Giuliani was instantly visible and present among the grieving people of New York. His caring was evident for the city's police and firefighters who risked their lives that horrible day. Giuliani became a symbol of a New York that cared and a mayor who exuded confidence that the city would overcome the worst disaster in its history.

While a crisis like 9/11 may be the ultimate test of your courage as a leader, it's not one you can anticipate. But you can be ready for the unexpected by being grounded in your True North and being clear about your beliefs and your principles. When you approach public issues from that point of view, instead of worrying about your image and the impressions you create, people respect you as a leader they can count on and will make sacrifices for the good of the whole.

BEING TRANSPARENT

The key to handling public issues is to be open, straightforward, and transparent. In a crisis, both employees and external observers are extremely sensitive to any attempts to dissemble or hide the truth. These will quickly be exposed, especially if subsequent events reveal your statements to be inaccurate or misleading.

Externally, you should offer access to the media, customers, shareholders, and other constituencies who have a stake in the company's future. I have found members of the media to be quite respectful when they believe you are telling them the whole story and not trying to cover up problems or ugly details. When they feel leaders are not shooting straight with them, they become aggressive and publish even the most far-fetched rumors and allegations.

Being transparent creates an open and human image of the organization. Its leaders seem like normal people who are tasked to take on difficult challenges. When you are open, you are in a better position to ask people for their support. If things get worse, as they often do, people are more sympathetic to your point of view if you have kept them fully informed. During this time, you should be highly accessible within your organization, wandering around the offices and labs, visiting factories, and participating in events around the company.

One new CEO, John Lechleiter of pharmaceutical giant Eli Lilly, writes a personal blog every few weeks that goes to all employees worldwide. He receives hundreds of e-mails in response and takes time personally to respond. Lechleiter has found his blogs have opened up a positive relationship with Lilly employees around the world, giving the company a more human image.

Why aren't more leaders comfortable with transparency? It takes time, its sheer informality may be subject to misinterpretation, and it offers potential fodder for plaintiffs' attorneys, the media, and other outside groups to use against the company. Thus, it requires greater skill and entails greater risk than more formal approaches. On balance, however, these risks are substantially outweighed by the benefits.

Of course, there are limits to transparency, such as release of classified or confidential information that would benefit your competitors. But they shouldn't be used as an excuse for withholding vital information the public needs.

BLENDING INTERNAL AND EXTERNAL COMMUNICATIONS

In today's world, internal and external communications have morphed into one, making it impossible to draw a bright line between them. Whatever is said inside the company is quickly transmitted to outsiders, and whatever is written or said outside is also read or heard inside. Therefore, communicating the same messages internally and externally is essential.

Being candid is no guarantee that you're not going to inadvertently create problems for yourself. I learned this lesson the hard way in the late 1990s. At a Medtronic chairman's briefing, I shared the status of the business with three hundred colleagues in person and many more watching on satellite. When I returned to my office, I noticed my remarks had appeared on Reuters in the midst of my talk. Unfortunately, Reuters got the story wrong because it went out *before* I was halfway through the explanation.

As CEO of Goldman Sachs, Hank Paulson was very open. With the firm making sharp cutbacks in early 2003 due to the dot-com collapse, he told security analysts at a conference that he felt confident that further savings could be made without hurting the firm. In a statement he quickly regretted, Paulson opined, "Twenty percent of the people at Goldman create 80 percent of the value." His statements were quickly picked up online and used against the firm by competitors. That set off a firestorm within Goldman, which prided itself on teamwork and the value of every employee. Paulson didn't duck the criticism. The next morning, he sent a voice mail to thirty thousand Goldman employees worldwide, apologizing for his comments and reiterating the value of every employee's contributions.

As treasury secretary in the midst of the global financial crisis, Paulson took the heat when things weren't going well. In doing so, he protected his boss, President George W. Bush, and Federal Reserve colleagues Ben Bernanke and Timothy Geithner from criticism, although they had been full participants in every decision. In spite of occasional missteps and not infrequent criticism, Paulson built his leadership around honesty and courage—traits that served him well throughout his career.

DEALING WITH WHISTLE-BLOWERS

How should you deal with whistle-blowers who communicate confidential company information to outside attorneys and government officials? In some cases, blowing the whistle is the only way well-intentioned employees have to reveal dishonest dealings within the company's hierarchy. In other cases, these allegations may be misleading or even untrue but reported as factual in the media.

Given these complexities, how should leaders deal with potential whistle-blowers? They can make them irrelevant by creating an open organization in which information flows freely and disgruntled employees have vehicles inside the company to express their concerns. Medtronic has made effective use of a confidential hot line that employees use to report their concerns anonymously. We used a formal procedure to follow up on these concerns and determine their validity and actions that were indicated.

In one case, an anonymous employee at a newly acquired subsidiary revealed instances of fraud being committed on the Food and Drug Administration (FDA) prior to the Medtronic acquisition. A preliminary investigation showed that the concerns were accurate. This finding was immediately reported to the FDA and action taken to withdraw the subsidiary's products from the market. We never did learn who made this report, but this internal whistle-blower did Medtronic a great favor. The FDA was appreciative that Medtronic turned itself in and took immediate action to correct the problem.

CREATING A CULTURE OF CANDOR

In *Transparency* Warren Bennis, Daniel Goleman, and James O'Toole write about the importance of creating "a culture of candor." Where such a culture does not exist, information doesn't flow freely through the organization, and its leaders often don't know what is going on. The only way to create such a culture is for leaders to be candid themselves. Then they can insist that people within their organizations be equally candid in bringing problems to them.

As the leader, you need to keep people informed of what's going on. The greater your openness, the more people will rely on you to provide them with the inside view, and the less they will rely on the rumor mill. If they cannot get the answers they need from the leaders, they will join the rumor mill.

PUBLIC CONFIDENCE, PRIVATE DOUBTS

Leaders in the public eye are expected to have the answers to most things. But what should you say when you don't know, which is usually the case at the outset of a crisis? This early period, when information is sketchy and people are trying to piece together the full story, can be an uncomfortable time. People are counting on you as the leader to reassure them that everything will be all right. That's hard to do when you don't know if the actual situation may be much worse than anyone imagines. How can you instill public confidence when you have private doubts?

The natural instinct of most leaders is to follow the advice of their lawyers and public relations specialists to hunker down until they know where they stand. By saying nothing internally or externally or issuing meaningless statements, leaders come across as being isolated from reality, insensitive and uncaring, or even as stonewalling. Worse yet, they may lose the initiative to outsiders prone to rash statements that contain elements of truth. Rumors start to spread inside and outside the organization. What could have been a manageable crisis suddenly develops into one careening out of control.

In an era of instant media focus on disasters and problems, the hunker-down strategy won't fly. Leaders are compelled to get out in front of the story immediately or abdicate their opportunities. You are better off seizing the initiative and telling people what you know and what you don't, while assuring them that others are working to get the facts as quickly as possible.

Karl Weick uses an incident from Warren Bennis's career to illustrate what he terms "the legitimation of doubt." Bennis was giving a lecture at the Harvard School of Education when Dean Paul Ylvisaker asked him, "Warren, do you really love being president of [the University of] Cincinnati?" After a long silence, Bennis responded, "I don't know."

On the flight back to Cincinnati the next day, Bennis ruminated over Ylvisaker's question. He finally admitted to himself that he didn't love being a university president. Two months later he announced his resignation.

What would have happened had Bennis continued in a job he didn't love? No one can answer that question for sure, not even Bennis. We do know he would not have been nearly as productive or insightful in his writing as he has been over the past thirty years. By resigning from a job he didn't like and instead doing what he loved, Bennis has not only had a more fulfilling life but has touched the lives of millions of people.

There are times in the life of every leader when you really don't know. Few have the courage to be as honest as Bennis was. They fear appearing ignorant, uncertain, or, worse yet, out of control. With the rapid pace of change and instant media events, doubt is a legitimate feeling. In fact, acknowledging that you don't know is far healthier than pretending you are certain. It validates the uncertainty that others are feeling and permits leaders to seek to understand, without committing themselves prematurely.

There is no need to draw premature conclusions about the cause of problems. Subsequent events may cause you to reverse your conclusions or dig yourself into a deep hole of an unreliable position. More important, you need to exude confidence that you are committed to finding out what happened and taking responsibility for the consequences.

WHO'S RESPONSIBLE FOR THIS CRISIS?

In 2007 Robert Eckert, CEO of Mattel Toys, received reports from consumers indicating lead in its toys. Subsequent testing in Mattel's laboratories revealed that lead exceeded permissible levels on a wide range of Mattel toys. This led to a series of recalls involving millions of toys. In its recall notices, Mattel made it clear that the toys were manufactured under contract by Chinese suppliers.

In testifying before Congress on September 11, 2007, Eckert placed the blame squarely on the Chinese contract manufacturers. "Contractor's failure to follow well established rules forced the recall of millions of toys with lead paint," he said. This resulted in a public outcry against Chinese manufacturers and their lack of standards for child safety. Senator Sam Brownbeck fanned the flames, saying, "Made in China has now become a warning label." Subsequently the owner of one of Mattel's suppliers committed suicide.

This raised the question, who was responsible for the defective toys: Mattel or its contract manufacturers? After several weeks of uninterrupted public outcry against the Chinese, Mattel's executive vice president finally apologized to the Chinese minister for shifting the criticism to China. He told the minister, "Mattel takes full responsibility for these recalls and apologizes personally to you, the Chinese people."

In the minds of U.S. consumers, Chinese-made products, on which Mattel and every other toy company depend for manufacturing, were tainted as unsafe. Since Mattel's name was on the toys and the company was responsible for certifying the toys met safety standards, Eckert should have immediately accepted responsibility. By denying Mattel's culpability and attempting to shift the blame to Chinese contract manufacturers, Eckert set off a wave of xenophobia in the United States. In the end, he hurt himself and his company's reputation much more than if he had accepted responsibility in the first place.

A VALENTINE'S DAY
TO REMEMBER

On Valentine's Day 2007, David Neeleman, the founder of JetBlue, faced the greatest crisis of his professional life. An East Coast ice storm stranded JetBlue passengers on the runway on nine flights up to ten hours. In the following days, over one thousand flights were cancelled. Although other airlines suffered similar problems, the negative press coverage focused on JetBlue, which had built its reputation on superior customer service.

Since Neeleman's expertise was in marketing, he had delegated day-to-day operations to chief operating officer Dave Barger. However, Barger was in Florida when the storm hit and remained there for the next several days. Operating without his long-time COO at his side, Neeleman spent the next week in JetBlue's operations center, trying to help his young managers get back on track.

It would have been natural for Neeleman to blame the ice storm for JetBlue's Valentine's Day catastrophe. Instead, he dug into the operational aspects of the business and realized that his young, growing airline did not have the systems and trained people to cope with major problems. "This was an operational failure," he said. "We had an emergency control center full of people who didn't know what to do because they lacked the systems and were ill equipped to handle a crisis of this magnitude."

To overhaul its operations, Neeleman convinced Russell Chew, COO of the Federal Aviation Administration, to join JetBlue. "Chew got things back on track, and kept them there," he noted with pride.

At the same time, Neeleman focused on restoring the confidence of JetBlue's customers by apologizing directly to them in a video. In the following week, he appeared on *David Letterman* and the *Today Show*. He even posted a video on YouTube.

Neeleman accepted responsibility for bad decisions and promised refunds and credits for the aggrieved passengers. He apologized repeatedly. Then he took a step unprecedented in the airline industry by announcing a customer bill of rights, committing JetBlue to spend $30 million to compensate passengers who had been stranded during the storm.

Not all stories have happy endings. Some of Neeleman's board members felt he went too far in publicly apologizing for the airline's operational shortcomings and also held him accountable for the operational failures. As a result, the board asked him to resign as CEO while promoting Barger to this role. The following year, Neeleman left the airline he founded to start a new low-cost Brazilian airline—ironically named Azul, or blue in Portuguese.

Neeleman's approach to JetBlue's crisis contrasts sharply with that of Mattel's Eckert. While Eckert denied his company's responsibility for its problems, Neeleman was able to get to the root cause by personally digging into the problem. Then he took steps to make permanent corrections. By publicly owning his organization's responsibility for the problems, Neeleman quickly regained the confidence of his customers.

Credit David Neeleman for saving JetBlue and its reputation. He may have lost his job, but he kept his integrity. Neeleman's approach takes a lot of courage—but isn't that what leading in crisis is all about?

LESSON LEARNED

These days the intensity of the spotlight is so great that leaders cannot get away with dissembling or being intentionally misleading. There are so many different channels for information to become public that the truth will eventually come to the surface. The velocity of information transmission is so fast that leaders must establish the groundwork for transparent communications long before the crisis hits. The key is getting out in front of the crisis in its first hours with clear statements, both internally and externally, that accept responsibility and build confidence and credibility with all your constituents.

Surviving a crisis is only half of the challenge. The greater opportunity belongs to leaders who use a crisis to transform their industries by staying focused on winning.

LESSON #7

GO ON OFFENSE, FOCUS ON WINNING NOW

Thus far, we have been examining ways to get through a crisis successfully. This is only half of the challenge. Now that we have learned to play defense, it's time to go on offense and focus on winning, not just getting through the crisis.

Look at a crisis as a gift. It provides you a golden opportunity that may not come again to reshape your business and your industry and emerge as the winner. But you've got to be bold and focused to seize it.

Many leaders assume if they can just get through a crisis, everything will return to normal. So they hunker down and wait for the storm to pass. In the meantime, their competitors are reshaping the market to their advantage.

Emerging from a crisis, markets never look the same as they did going into it. People on Wall Street who are waiting for the glory days of 2006–2007 to return with high fees and even higher leverage may have a long wait. High profits will return, but the means of making money will be entirely different than it was.

Why not reshape the market yourself? First, you need a clear vision of what future markets will look like. This requires a keen understanding of how your customers' needs will change as a result of the crisis. Second, you need a focused strategy to reshape markets to play to your strengths while exposing your competitors' weaknesses.

Then you've got to move aggressively to put your strategies into action, just as forcefully as you did to survive the crisis. If you can pull this off, you may be able to catch your competitors off guard. By the time they wake up to what your organization is doing, you will have solidified your leadership of the post-crisis market.

TRANSFORM THE MARKET— AND YOUR COMPANY

Let's look at several visionary leaders who have used a looming crisis to reshape their business and their markets: PepsiCo's Indra Nooyi, IBM's Sam Palmisano, Infosys's Narayana Murthy, and Apple's Steve Jobs.

Indra Nooyi
In May 2009 PepsiCo CEO Indra Nooyi made a profound speech about the new breed of CEOs and their responsibility to society. "The hard-edged leader, delivering return on capital at no matter what emotional or social cost, is yesterday's leader,"

she said. "The new breed of CEO has to create sustainable value. A company is granted a license to operate from society and therefore owes society a duty of care. Pursuit of short-term performance is not enough. That performance needs to be allied to a purpose; otherwise, the performance disappears too."

To Nooyi, these were not just words but the hallmark of her leadership at PepsiCo. Promoted to CEO in August 2006, India-born Nooyi immediately recognized that PepsiCo was facing difficult social issues. She anticipated rising concerns about obesity, diabetes, and the availability of clean water, coupled with the move to healthy foods. Rather than resisting these trends, she turned them into the vision that she is using to reinvent PepsiCo: "Performance with Purpose."

Nooyi knew that PepsiCo had to broaden its business beyond sugar-based drinks and high-calorie snack foods, which accounted for the vast majority of its profits. As *U.S. News* noted in her 2008 selection for America's Best Leaders, she is taking the company "from snack food to health food, from caffeine colas to fruit juices, and from shareholder value to sustainable enterprise." Nooyi has her people working on new products that appeal to health-conscious consumers in beverages and snacks, building off energy-based drinks like Gatorade and the True North line of healthy snacks.

She didn't stop there. She committed PepsiCo to generate half of its U.S. revenues from healthy foods, to campaign against obesity, and to give $16 million to bring safe water to developing countries, as well as conserving 5 billion liters of water in its operations. Nooyi has positioned PepsiCo to ride the trends rather than swimming against them, and to be a positive force in addressing major social concerns. She has unified her global organization around these strategies and the values implicit in them. That's why she is a role model for the twenty-first-century CEO.

Sam Palmisano

When Sam Palmisano was elected CEO of IBM in 2003, he replaced an iconic leader in Lou Gerstner. Palmisano, who has spent his entire career with IBM, recognized the daunting task that remained to rebuild IBM. He neither tried to emulate Gerstner nor did he reverse direction on his gains.

Instead of waiting for the challenges of globalization to have an impact on IBM, Palmisano anticipated where globalization and technology were headed. Based on that vision, he reshaped IBM's strategy to become a total systems supplier to meet the evolving needs of its global customers, with emphasis on services, not hardware.

Palmisano also wanted IBM employees to focus on "leading by values." Rather than reinforcing IBM's historical values from the top down, he initiated a "values jam." This event gave all IBM employees around the world the opportunity to go online over a seventy-two-hour period and contribute to selecting IBM's values.

The bottom-up process yielded IBM's three new core values: dedication to every client's success, innovation, and trust.

As a result, Palmisano was able to gain the commitment of IBM employees to these values. In the words of 1960s marketing guru Marshall McLuhan, "The medium is the message." Palmisano used the medium of IBM's own network technology to engage employees in creating a broadly supported message.

He also reshaped the mammoth IBM global organization of 344,000 employees away from geographical and product silos into the "globally integrated enterprise." In a carefully crafted 2006 article in *Foreign Affairs* magazine, Palmisano laid out the case for an organization that paralleled the needs of its global customers with a weblike structure that looked more like the Internet than the traditional hierarchy IBM had deployed for decades.

In 2006 Palmisano got the opportunity to demonstrate IBM's new global capabilities when it landed a massive commitment to provide a new information and communications system for one of the world's largest banks, Industrial and Commercial Bank of China (ICBC). Along with Goldman Sachs, IBM helped ICBC restructure its far-flung network of fifty thousand loosely connected branches into eighteen thousand centers, all connected by the new IBM system. The chairman of ICBC proudly told me that it was the largest computer network ever installed in China. "We could not have accomplished it without Mr. Palmisano's commitment," he said.

In his early years as CEO, Palmisano was criticized for not getting IBM's stock price up. He recognized then that the strategic and cultural changes he was implementing would take five to seven years to yield results. Since the start of the global economic crisis, IBM has been one of the few technology companies to produce consistent increases in its earnings and shareholder value. Palmisano's ability to anticipate the pending globalization crisis enabled his company to come out of it a big winner.

Narayana Murthy

At thirty-five years old, Narayana Murthy founded Bangalore-based Infosys with five colleagues from his former company. Starting with an investment of less than one hundred dollars, Murthy envisioned that his custom software firm would become "India's most respected company." Murthy explained how hard it was getting started in 1981. "It was a crisis throughout," he said. "We were forced to finance growth out of our earnings, but that instilled discipline. The hardships and financial challenges didn't sap our enthusiasm."

Because Murthy refused to pay a bribe to telephone installers, Infosys waited an entire year to get its telephone line installed. "What drains your energy is not the fiscal problem, but violating your value system," said Murthy. "We always believed the softest pillow is a clear conscience. If you refuse to buckle down on the first couple of transactions, they go after someone else."

Every company comes close to death at least once in its early years, and Infosys was no exception. It faced a near-death experience in 1989 when U.S. visa restrictions made it impossible to send its programmers to U.S. customer locations. Compounding Infosys's problems, the Indian government relaxed its trade restrictions, permitting multinational giants like IBM to reenter the country.

Believing that Infosys was as good as dead, one of its founders quit, and the others were deeply shaken. Murthy was so committed that he offered to buy out any founder who wanted to sell. That turned the tide. As one cofounder said, "If you are staying on, then I'm with you." Later Murthy admitted he didn't have the money to buy anyone out.

Necessity is the mother of virtue. The crisis caused Murthy to develop a new strategy to compete directly with the giants by matching or exceeding their software quality. Infosys leveraged its access to a pool of low-cost, highly skilled talent, which it recruited with a stimulating work environment and equity-based compensation. Murthy's strategy was wildly successful. From fewer than 100 employees, Infosys has grown to more than 100,000 employees and has a market capitalization of $10 billion, all due to Narayana Murthy's courage in the face of crisis.

Steve Jobs

Apple founder Steve Jobs had similar success after returning as CEO in 1997. Jobs founded Apple in 1976 at the age of twenty-one and pioneered the personal computer with products like Macintosh, known for its color graphics and friendly user interface. He was ousted in 1985 in a power struggle with CEO John Sculley. As it turned out, Apple was the one that struggled in Jobs' twelve-year hiatus. Meanwhile, Jobs founded

NeXT Computer and acquired Pixar, where he created eleven highly acclaimed animated films.

Jobs returned after Apple bought NeXT and Pixar was sold to Walt Disney. Recognizing that IBM-clone personal computers had the corporate computing network locked up, Jobs revolutionized his company and the music world with iPod and iTunes. Now he is changing the mobile phone market with the iPhone.

At each stage of his amazing journey, Jobs used his creative genius—first in computing, then in filmmaking, and more recently in music and telephony—to transform entire industries and become the leader by leveraging Apple's innovative capabilities in color graphics and user interface.

Each of these leaders had the vision to see what changes were coming in their markets. Based on these changes, they designed unique strategies that played to their company's strengths to enable them to go on the offensive. In that way, they minimized the impact of the crisis and established themselves as the leaders in their emerging markets. That gave them the advantage over competitors that were still focusing on negative impact of the crisis on their existing markets.

INVEST DURING DOWNTURNS

Visionary companies gear their businesses for the long term by preparing for sharp economic swings so that they can invest during the downturns. They recognize that competitors are likely to pull back investments when the economy turns down and markets decline. Well aware of the lead time for capital investments, they know they must invest heavily in downturns or they won't be ready for the upswing. That takes substantial cash balances to withstand downturns while funding the expanded investments.

Two companies that rigorously follow this strategy are Intel and Exxon, both in capital-intensive industries with long lead times. In the 1980s, Intel and Motorola were running neck-and-neck in the microprocessor business. When the economy turned down in the late 1980s, Intel invested heavily in the Pentium microprocessors and added advanced wafer fabrication facilities to manufacture at lower cost. Motorola was forced to make major cutbacks in capital spending due to limited cash flow. When demand for microprocessors turned up, Motorola was caught flatfooted by Intel's new products. As a result, Intel was able to capture over 80 percent market share of microprocessors, while Motorola eventually divested its microprocessor business.

In 1999 Exxon purchased Mobil Oil at the bottom of the price cycle, when oil cost only $9 per barrel. Exxon preserved its cash by issuing stock to complete the $80 billion transaction, the largest ever at that point. Synergies produced by the merger turned Exxon into an enormous cash generator, which enabled the company to expand capital expenditures while repurchasing all the stock issued for the transaction.

Nor did Exxon management flinch in 2009 as the price of oil plummeted from $147 per barrel in June 2008 to nearly $40 in the spring of 2009. Its executive team had seen these cycles before and was prepared for the worst, yet ready to take advantage of solid long-term investments as opportunities arose. Even with profits receding from 2008's high levels, Exxon announced in April 2009 that it planned to spend $29 billion on capital in 2009, up from $15 billion in 2005. Meanwhile, many of Exxon's competitors pulled back from major projects to preserve cash.

The success of Intel and Exxon over many decades provides evidence of the importance of leadership that keeps its strategies and its organization keenly focused on the long term and does not get drawn off course by economic swings and near-term events.

7 STEPS TO FOCUS ON WINNING

How do you take the global economic crisis, or any other crisis, and turn it into an opportunity to transform your markets and your company? Here are 7 steps to keep your organization focused on winning in the depth of the crisis:

- *Step 1: Rethink your industry strategy.* To figure out what your markets will look like after the crisis requires a keen understanding of the changing needs of your customers. One

7 STEPS TO FOCUS ON WINNING

Step 1   Rethink your Industry strategy.

Step 2   Shed your weaknesses.

Step 3   Reshape the industry to play to your strengths.

Step 4   Make vital investments during the downturn.

Step 5   Keep key people focused on winning.

Step 6   Create your company's image as the industry leader.

Step 7   Develop rigorous execution plans.

example from the current crisis is the extent to which consumers have shifted from expensive luxury goods to more practical items. That's why high-end department stores like Neiman Marcus and Saks have fared poorly. Even fashion-forward discounters like Target have not done well. This doesn't necessarily mean consumers have lost their interest in upscale merchandise. Rather than returning to these same stores after the crisis, are consumers more likely to be attracted to chic low-cost items and trendy value-oriented merchandise? If this turns out to be the case, how can your company take advantage of shifts like these?

- *Step 2: Shed your weaknesses.* A crisis presents the opening to eliminate your organization's weaknesses, especially if it is too bureaucratic or too slow-moving to be competitive. That's what CEO Anne Mulcahy did in cutting twenty-eight thousand jobs to enable Xerox to become competitive once again. Now she is refocusing Xerox, long known as the plain paper copier company, on the paperless, all-digital office. How can you use your crisis to shed your organization's weaknesses to prepare for future competition? You will never have a better opportunity.

- *Step 3: Reshape the industry to play to your strengths.* The bold strategy coming out of a crisis is to move your entire industry to make your strengths the basis for competition while exposing your competitors' weaknesses. That's what IBM, Apple, and Medtronic did. What strategies can you deploy to expose your competitor's weaknesses? How can you shift the market to value your strengths? In recent years, we have learned that using size to be all things to all people doesn't work. To win in the emerging market, you need a highly focused strategy that builds off your unique strengths.

- *Step 4: Make vital investments during the downturn.* Intel and Exxon offer evidence that you cannot wait to make vital investments you need to win in the emerging market. When it appeared growth was slowing in the pharmaceutical industry, Novartis CEO Dan Vasella made counterintuitive moves by expanding Novartis's generic drug, vaccines, and consumer health businesses in spending heavily on acquisitions to offer alternatives to patented drugs. Meanwhile, he focused Novartis's pharmaceutical businesses more on targeted specialty drugs. What investments must you make at the depths of the downturn to emerge as the leader? Can you think the unthinkable and invest in a new strategic thrust when you're on your knees? It takes courage to defy conventional thinking and launch a bold new strategy when business is bad.

• *Step 5: Keep key people focused on winning.* During a crisis there's a risk that your entire organization gets so focused on keeping the ship afloat that no one is planning ahead. Therefore, you should assign a small team of highly talented people to devise the postcrisis strategy. It may seem risky to pull key people out of crisis management to plan for the future, but this is required to win. How will you reshape your organization's strategy to emerge from the crisis as the winner?

• *Step 6: Create your company's image as the industry leader.* With public criticism of Wall Street mounting and the industry defending itself, emerging financial service leaders are envisioning changes needed in capital markets. In a major policy address in April 2009, Goldman's Lloyd Blankfein outlined industry-wide changes required to restore sound risk taking, provide appropriate regulation, focus accounting on marking-to-market, and establish long-term compensation practices that reward sustainable gains. How can you recreate your company's image to be the emerging leader that understands customer needs in the new environment?

• *Step 7: Develop rigorous execution plans.* This final step is often overlooked by visionary leaders who devise new strategies but fail to underpin them with detailed plans for marketplace execution. Emergent strategies are only as good as their execution. Sound execution requires not only attention to detailed planning, but adaptability to changing market conditions to alter tactics to meet customer needs. How effective is your organization in executing its plans? Do you assign your best people to this task and measure them in minute detail? Are your plans flexible enough to adapt to changing market conditions, while still maintaining discipline? If the answer to all three questions is affirmative, then you are well positioned to come out of this crisis as the winner in your market.

Following these 7 steps with clarity and rigor will enable your organization to emerge from the crises you face as a leader in your field. By going on the offense, you can gain competitive advantage and build your market position to sustain your future growth and success.

LESSON LEARNED

The final lesson to be learned is to keep your head up during a crisis rather than hunkering down, and maintain a laser-like focus on winning in the emerging marketplace. This period offers the best opportunity you will ever have to reshape markets to your advantage.

The best leaders emerge from a crisis as winners because they are both aggressive and courageous in turning the challenges to their advantage. Beyond that, they are passionate about using their leadership to make a difference in the world.

CONCLUSION

CRISIS MAY BE YOUR DEFINING MOMENT

Until one is committed there is always hesitancy,

The chance to draw back, always ineffectiveness . . .

The moment one definitely commits oneself, then providence moves too.

All sorts of things occur to help that never otherwise would have occurred. . .

Whatever you can do or dream you can, begin it.

Boldness has genius, power and magic in it.

—W. H. Murray

The crisis you are facing, or inevitably will face, may be the defining moment in your professional life. Scottish mountain climber Murray's wisdom offers a powerful message to today's leaders as you face that moment: get committed to a bold plan, and the universe will move with you to enable you to turn your dream into reality.

In *The Defining Moment*, Jonathan Alter describes the defining moment in the life of President Franklin D. Roosevelt. Taking office at the height of the Great Depression, Roosevelt inherited a collapsing economy: 25 percent of Americans were unemployed, banks had shut down in thirty-four states, and business investment was down 90 percent.

On his first full day in office, March 5, 1933, Roosevelt recognized that the responsibility to save the country rested squarely on his shoulders. In his inaugural address the previous day, Roosevelt had offered the American people these reassuring words: "The only thing we have to fear is fear itself." By the next day, he was anything but reassured. Roosevelt rose to the challenge to lead the country out of the depression and later guided the Allied forces through World War II to defeat Nazi Germany and Japan.

Winston Churchill's leadership during World War II is another classic example of a leader confronting a crisis that became his defining moment. Reflecting on his darkest time during the Battle of Britain, Churchill said, "I felt as if I were walking with destiny, and that all my past life had been but preparation for this hour."

Many have written that President Barack Obama faced a similar set of circumstances on January 21, 2009, when he took the oath of office. While that may be true, I believe the defining moment of Obama's professional life occurred on March 18, 2008.

For days Obama had been under severe attack by conservative commentators and rival Hillary Clinton for his association with his radical pastor, Reverend Jeremiah Wright. Night after night, cable television channels ran clips of Wright's sermons in endless loops that raised racial fears across the country. As much as Americans want to bury racial differences in our society, those fears and the racial divide lie just beneath the surface, whether we admit it or not.

Thus far, Obama had not brought his race into the campaign. Now he recognized he could no longer avoid the issue. Racial fears threatened to sink his campaign for president just as he was gaining traction against Senator Clinton.

Obama did not flinch. He decided to confront the issue head-on by making a major address in Philadelphia in the shadow of Constitution Hall. He squarely faced Americans' fears while describing his own mixed-race history. Then he took the discussion to a higher plane by proposing a unifying theme in order to achieve a more perfect union:

> We cannot solve the challenges of our time unless we solve them together—unless we perfect our union by understanding that we may have different stories, but we hold common hopes. . . . We all want to move in the same direction—toward a better future for our children and our grandchildren.

MY DEFINING MOMENT

My defining moment came in 1988 on a beautiful fall day in Minnesota, with the maple trees ablaze in reds and oranges. Driving around the lake near our home, I looked in the rearview mirror and saw a person in agony who was in the midst of a crisis and drifting away from his True North.

I asked myself, *How could this be?* In my wife, Penny, I had an amazing life partner of twenty years, two wonderful sons, and a great job as executive vice president of Minneapolis's leading company.

What I saw in that mirror was a person striving so hard to become CEO of a large company like Honeywell that he was rapidly abandoning his True North. I was getting caught up in the politics and appearances at Honeywell, which were rampant at the time, rather than ignoring them as I had in the past. I was even wearing cufflinks to impress senior people, something I had never done before.

In that instant, I recognized that Honeywell was not the right place for me and that I was not proud of what was happening to me in this environment. That was the defining moment when I decided to stop striving to become CEO of Honeywell and to get back to focusing on values-centered leadership.

I drove home and told Penny what I was feeling. She said wisely, "I've been trying to tell you this for a year, but you weren't prepared to hear it." How right she was. Often it is the person closest to us who looks through our blind spots and sees us as we really are.

Just three months before, I had turned Medtronic down for the third time in ten years to become its president, most likely because the company wasn't large enough to fit my image of what I should be doing. When I walked through Medtronic's front door six months later as its new president, I felt as if I was coming home—home to an organization where I had never been before. It felt like home, a place where I could grow personally and make a difference in helping to fulfill our shared mission of "restoring people to full life and health."

Everything that has happened in my professional life in the past twenty years followed from that decision, from my thirteen years at Medtronic to my focus the last seven years on helping leaders develop themselves.

. . . AND YOURS

What is your defining moment? When that moment arrives, will you be prepared to heed your calling to step up and lead?

Your defining moment comes when your life story collides with a crisis in the midst of your path. It is in this crisis that you learn who you really are. When you are under enormous pressure and the consequences are greatest for you, will you be prepared to follow your True North?

Is the crisis you are facing right now your defining moment? In leading people through these challenges, what are you learning about yourself? Are you being true to your beliefs and your values? Or have you buckled under the pressures or been pulled off course by the seductions of the moment? In answering these questions, you are defining the authenticity of your leadership.

This moment defines you to others as well. People remember how leaders respond in a crisis because intuitively they know this is the authentic test of the person. That's why people acknowledge New York Mayor Rudy Giuliani for his leadership following the attacks of September 11. In like manner, people recall Richard Fuld as the leader only when Lehman went bankrupt, not as the successful executive who built the organization for thirty years.

In a crisis, people look to leaders' hearts and their humanity, not just the brilliance of their minds. In *A Sense of Urgency*, John Kotter writes, "People who see opportunity in a crisis . . . recognize that the biggest single problem of all is in the heart where fear and anger can kill hope. They recognize that the heart needs hope, they tend to act with passion, with conviction, with optimism, and with a steely resolve. . . . They focus on others' hearts much more than on their minds."

MAKING A DIFFERENCE IN THE WORLD

In 1966 Robert F. Kennedy said, "Few will have the greatness to bend history itself. But each of us can work to change a small portion of events, and in the total of all these acts will be written the history of this generation."

It may not be our destiny to bend history as Roosevelt and Churchill did. But each of us has the opportunity to make a difference in the world by leading others through crises to change a small portion of events. If we learn our leadership lessons well, the history of this new generation will most assuredly be a great one.

The world is crying out for your leadership. We face six major problems that are so pressing that we must address them now: global peace, health care, energy and the environment, job creation, income disparities, and education. These problems are so large and intractable that no one organization can possibly solve them on its own. That's why they require each of us to use our leadership gifts to contribute to changing a small portion of these problems. Anthropologist Margaret Mead once said, "Never doubt the power of a small group of people to change the world. Indeed, it is the only thing that ever has."

How can your leadership of your group help resolve these problems and others you see in your midst? Don't try to do it overnight. Instead, get committed to lead people to change a small portion of these events, and providence will move with you. And you will become one of the authors of a bright future for this generation.

The time is ripe for you to step up and lead people through the current crisis. Be bold in your leadership because boldness has genius, power, and magic in it. If you stay on course of your True North, you can make a lasting difference in the world.

This is the ultimate fulfillment of leading people through a crisis.

APPENDIX

Leaders Featured in
7 Lessons for Leading in Crisis

Leader	Title and Organization
Dave Barger	Chairman and CEO, JetBlue
Warren Bennis	University professor, University of Southern California
Ben Bernanke	Chair, U.S. Federal Reserve Bank
Lloyd Blankfein	Chair and CEO, Goldman Sachs
John Bogle	Founder, Vanguard
John Hope Bryant	Founder, Operation HOPE
Warren Buffett	Chair and CEO, Berkshire Hathaway
Jim Burke	Former chair and CEO, Johnson and Johnson
George W. Bush	Past president, United States
Richard Cheney	Past vice president, United States
Russell Chew	Chief operating officer, JetBlue
Winston Churchill	Former prime minister, United Kingdom
Hillary Clinton	U.S. secretary of state
Gerhard Cromme	Chair, supervisory board, Siemens
Max DePree	Former CEO, Herman Miller
Jamie Dimon	Chair and CEO, J. P. Morgan
Robert Eckert	Chair and CEO, Mattel Toys

Carly Fiorina	Former chair and CEO, Hewlett-Packard
Richard Fuld	Former chair and CEO, Lehman
Timothy Geithner	U.S. treasury secretary
David Gergen	Director, Center for Public Leadership, Harvard Kennedy School
Lou Gerstner	Former chair and CEO, IBM
Ray Gilmartin	Former chair and CEO, Merck
Rudy Giuliani	Former mayor, New York City
Hank Greenberg	Former chair and CEO, AIG
Alan Greenspan	Former chair, U.S. Federal Reserve Bank
Andy Grove	Former chair and CEO, Intel
Bill Hawkins	Chair and CEO, Medtronic
Jeff Immelt	Chair and CEO, General Electric
Steve Jobs	Chair and CEO, Apple Computer
Andrea Jung	Chair and CEO, Avon
Klaus Kleinfeld	Chair and CEO, Alcoa
Wendy Kopp	Founder and president, Teach For America
Ken Lay	Former chair, Enron
John Lechleiter	Chair and CEO, Eli Lilly
Ed Liddy	Chair and CEO, AIG
Peter Loescher	President and CEO, Siemens
Terry Lundgren	Chair and CEO, Macy's
John Mack	Chair and CEO, Morgan Stanley
Philip McCrea	CEO, ClearPoint Learning
Robert McNamara	Former U.S. secretary of defense
Gordon Moore	Former chair and CEO, Intel
Alan Mulally	President and CEO, Ford Motor Company
Anne Mulcahy	Chair and CEO, Xerox
Narayana Murthy	Founder and chief learning officer, Infosys

David Neeleman	Former chair and CEO, JetBlue
Indra Nooyi	Chair and CEO, PepsiCo
Barack Obama	President, United States
Sam Palmisano	Chair and CEO, IBM
Vikram Pandit	Chair and CEO, Citigroup
Hank Paulson	Former U.S. Treasury secretary
Tad Piper	Former chair and CEO, Piper Jaffrey
Chuck Prince	Former chair and CEO, Citigroup
Philip Purcell	Former chair and CEO, Morgan Stanley
Franklin D. Roosevelt	Past president, United States
Robert Rubin	Former U.S. treasury secretary
Alan Schwartz	Former president and CEO, Bear Stearns
John Sculley	Former CEO, Apple Computer
Kevin Sharer	Chairman and CEO, Amgen
Gregg Steinhafel	Chairman and CEO, Target
Martin Sullivan	Former chair and CEO, AIG
Lawrence Summers	Economic advisor to U.S. president
Charles Thornton	Former chair and CEO, Litton Industries
Robert Ulrich	Chair and CEO, Target
Dan Vasella	Chair and CEO, Novartis
Heinrich von Pierer	Former chair and CEO, Siemens
Win Wallin	Former and CEO, Medtronic
Sherron Watkins	Former vice president, Enron
Jack Welch	Former chair and CEO, General Electric
Sandy Weill	Former chair and CEO, Citigroup
Oprah Winfrey	Founder and president, Harpo
Jerry York	Former CFO, IBM

REFERENCES

Introduction

Badaracco, J. L. Jr. *Questions of Character.* Boston: Harvard Business School Press, 2006, p. 100.

Bartlett, C., and McLean, A. *GE's Jeff Immelt: The Voyage from MBA to CEO.* Boston: Harvard Business School Publishing, June 2006.

Blankfein, L. "Address to the Council of Institutional Investors." Washington, D.C., Apr. 7, 2009.

Buffett, M., and Clark, D. *The Tao of Warren Buffett: Warren Buffett's Words of Wisdom: Quotations and Interpretations to Help Guide You to Billionaire Wealth and Enlightened Business Management.* New York: Scribner, 2006, p. 60.

Cohan, W. "A Tsunami of Excuses." *New York Times,* Mar. 11, 2009.

Friedman, M. "The Social Responsibility of Business Is to Increase Its Profits." *New York Times,* Sept. 13, 1970.

George, B. *Authentic Leadership: Rediscovering the Secrets to Creating Lasting Value.* San Francisco: Jossey-Bass, 2003.

George, B., with Sims, P. *True North.* San Francisco: Jossey-Bass, 2007.

Goodman, E. C., and Goodman, T. *The Forbes Book of Business Quotations: 14,266 Thoughts on the Business of Life.* New York: Black Dog & Leventhal Publishers, 1997, p. 11.

Guerrera, F. "Welch Denounces Corporate Obsessions." *Financial Times,* Mar. 13, 2009.

Lipton, M., Lorsch, J. W., and Mirvis, T. N. "Schumer's Shareholder Bill Misses the Mark." *Wall Street Journal,* May 12, 2009.

Lesson #1

Burke, E. *Reflections on the Revolution in France*. Stanford, Calif.: Stanford University Press, 2001.

DePree, M. *Leadership Is an Art*. New York: Dell Publishing, 1989, p. 11.

Dimon, J. "Crisis, Community, and Leadership." Address to the World Economic Forum Panel, Davos, Switzerland, Jan. 29, 2009.

George, B. *Kevin Sharer at Amgen: Sustaining the High-Growth Company (A)*. Boston: Harvard Business School Publishing, Sept. 2008.

George, B. *Kevin Sharer at Amgen: Sustaining the High-Growth Company (B)*. Boston: Harvard Business School Publishing, Sept. 2008.

George, W. *Philip McCrea: Once an Entrepreneur . . . (B)*. Boston: Harvard Business School Publishing, Apr. 2009.

George, W., and McLean, A. *Philip McCrea: Once an Entrepreneur . . . (A)*. Boston: Harvard Business School Publishing, Aug. 2008.

Paine, L. S., and Santoro M. A. *Forging the New Salomon*. Boston: Harvard Business School Publishing, Jan. 2004.

Simons, R. L., Rosenberg, K., and Kindred, N. *Merck: Managing Vioxx (A)*. Boston: Harvard Business School Publishing, Apr. 2009.

Simons, R. L., Rosenberg, K., and Kindred, N. *Merck: Managing Vioxx (B)*. Boston: Harvard Business School Publishing, Apr. 2009.

Lesson #2

Alcoholics Anonymous. "The Twelve Steps of Alcoholics Anonymous." 2009. http://www.aa.org/.

Bryant, J. H. *Love Leadership: The New Way to Lead in a Fear-Based World*. San Francisco: Jossey-Bass, 2009.

George, B. *Kevin Sharer at Amgen: Sustaining the High-Growth Company (A)*. Boston: Harvard Business School Publishing, Sept. 2008.

George, B. *Kevin Sharer at Amgen: Sustaining the High-Growth Company (B)*. Boston: Harvard Business School Publishing, Sept. 2008.

George, B., and McLean, A. *Anne Mulcahy: Leading Xerox Through the Perfect Storm*. Boston: Harvard Business School Publishing, Jan. 26, 2005.

George, B., and McLean, A. *Tad Piper and Piper Jaffray*. Boston: Harvard Business School Publishing, Oct. 2005.

"Piper Manager's Losses May Total $700 Million." *Wall Street Journal*, Aug. 25, 1994, pp. C1, C19.

Lesson #3

Bryant, A. "Knock-Knock: It's the C.E.O." *New York Times*, Apr. 11, 2009.

Hodges, D. *Quote This! A Collection of Illustrated Quotes for Educators.* Thousand Oaks, Calif.: Corwin Press, 2008, p. 71.

Tedlow, R., and Smith, W. *James Burke: A Career in American Business (A)*. Boston: Harvard Business School Publishing, Oct. 2005.

Tedlow, R., and Smith, W. *James Burke: A Career in American Business (B)*. Boston: Harvard Business School Publishing, Oct. 2005.

Winfrey, O. "Academy of Achievement Oprah Winfrey Interview." Chicago, Feb. 21, 1991.

Lesson #4

Bogle, J. C. "A Crisis of Ethic Proportions." *Wall Street Journal*, Apr. 20, 2009.

George, B., Mayer, D., and McLean, A. *Andrea Jung: Empowering Avon Women (A)*. Boston: Harvard Business School Publishing, July 2007.

George, B., Mayer, D., and McLean, A. *Andrea Jung: Empowering Avon Women (B)*. Boston: Harvard Business School Publishing, Jan. 2008.

Grove, A. *Only the Paranoid Survive: How to Exploit the Crisis Points That Challenge Every Company.* New York: Doubleday, 1996, pp. 88–89.

Kelly, K. "How Goldman Profited from Subprime Meltdown." *Wall Street Journal*, Sept. 17, 2007.

Mulcahy, A. "Xerox CEO Interviewed by Bill George." Presentation at Harvard Business School, Boston, Apr. 2005.

Lesson #5

George, W., Mayer, D., and McLean, A. *Wendy Kopp and Teach for America (A)*. Boston: Harvard Business School Publishing, Apr. 2007.

George, W., Mayer, D., and McLean, A. *Wendy Kopp and Teach for America (B)*. Boston: Harvard Business School Publishing, Apr. 2007.

Seelye, K. Q. "A Different Emanuel for One Church." *New York Times*, Mar. 17, 2009.

Vlasic, B. "Choosing Its Own Path, Ford Stayed Independent." *New York Times*, Apr. 8, 2009.

Lesson #6

Bennis, W., Goleman, D., and O'Toole, J. *Transparency: How Leaders Create a Culture of Candor.* San Francisco: Jossey-Bass, 2008.

Bennis, W., Spreitzer, G., and Cummings, T. (eds.) *The Future of Leadership: Today's Top Leadership Thinkers Speak to Tomorrow's Leaders.* San Francisco: Jossey-Bass, 2001.

Faler, B., and Burke, H. *Mattel's Eckert Blames Contractors for Toy Recalls.* Bloomberg.com, Sept. 12, 2007.

George, B., and Breitfelder, M. *David Neeleman: Flight Path of a Servant Leader (A).* Boston: Harvard Business School Publishing, July 2008.

George, B., and Breitfelder, M. *David Neeleman: Flight Path of a Servant Leader (B).* Boston: Harvard Business School Publishing, July 2008.

Lee, H., Tseng, M., and Hoyt, D. *Unsafe for Children: Mattel's Toy Recalls and Supply Chain Management.* Stanford, Calif.: Stanford Graduate School of Business.

Weisman, S. R., and Anderson, J. "Can Hank Paulson Defuse This Crisis?" *New York Times,* July 27, 2008.

Weick, K. "Leadership as the Legitimation of Doubt." In W. Bennis, G. Spreitzer, and T. Cummings (eds.), *The Future of Leadership: Today's Top Leadership Thinkers Speak to Tomorrow's Leaders.* San Francisco: Jossey-Bass, 2001.

Lesson #7

George, W., Singh, S., and McLean, A. *Narayana Murthy and Compassionate Capitalism.* Boston: Harvard Business School, June 2006.

McLuhan, M., and Fiore, Q. *The Medium Is the Message.* Berkeley, Calif.: Gingko Press, 1967.

Nooyi, I. "Leading to the Future." Speech to the Economic Club of Washington, D.C., May 13, 2009.

Palmisano, S. J. "The Globally Integrated Enterprise." *Foreign Affairs,* 2006, 85(3), 127–136.

Useem, M. "America's Best Leaders: Indra Nooyi, PepsiCo CEO." *U.S. News,* Nov. 19, 2008.

Conclusion

Alter, J. *The Defining Moment: FDR's Hundred Days and the Triumph of Hope.* New York: Simon & Schuster, 2006.

Churchill, W. S. *The Second World War, Vol. 1: The Gathering Storm.* Boston: Houghton Mifflin, 1948.

Kotter, J. P. *A Sense of Urgency.* Boston: Harvard Business Press, 2008.

Margaret Mead quotation attributed to her in *Christian Science Monitor,* June 1, 1989.

Murray, W. H. *The Scottish Himalayan Expedition.* London: J. M. Dent and Sond, 1951, pp. 6–7.

Obama, B. "A More Perfect Union." Speech in Philadelphia, Mar. 18, 2008.

Torricelli, R. G., Carroll, A., and Goodwin, D. K. *In Our Own Words: Extraordinary Speeches of the American Century.* New York: Simon and Schuster, 2000.

FURTHER STUDY OF
7 LESSONS FOR
LEADING IN CRISIS

To explore the 7 Lessons in greater depth, I recommend that you go to www.billgeorge.org for additional ideas and discussion about the lessons.

If you would like to discuss these ideas with colleagues at work or friends, you can receive your free study guide, "Leader's Guide to 7 Lessons for Leading in Crisis," by going to www.billgeorge.org.

To contact me directly about speaking opportunities or discussion of the 7 Lessons, please send an e-mail directly to me at bill@bpgeorge.com.

For leadership programs on the 7 Lessons, contact Nick Craig at the Authentic Leadership Institute Web site, www.auth leadership.com.